CW00521706

ANTICHRIST
A R I S I N G

MICHELE NEAL

GLOBAL CHAOS AND ITS PROPHESIED SOLUTION

ANTICHRIST
ARISING

FOREWORD BY
THE REVEREND CHARLYNNE M. BODDIE

Antichrist Arising – Global Chaos and its Prophesied Solution

Copyright © 2020 Michele Neal.

Graphic design and typesetting by JWC Creative. www.jwccreative.com

No part of this book shall be reproduced or transmitted in any form or by any means, electronic or mechanical, including photocopying, recording, or by any information retrieval system without written permission from the author.

The copyright notices below are listed in order of the quantity of scripture verses quoted from each Bible translation.

Scripture quotations marked AMP are taken from the Amplified® Bible (AMP), Copyright © 2015 by The Lockman Foundation. Used by permission. www.Lockman.org

Scripture quotations marked ESV are from The ESV® Bible (The Holy Bible, English Standard Version®), copyright © 2001 by Crossway, a publishing ministry of Good News Publishers. Used by permission. All rights reserved.

Scripture quotations marked NLT are taken from the Holy Bible, New Living Translation, copyright ©1996, 2004, 2015 by Tyndale House Foundation. Used by permission of Tyndale House Publishers, a Division of Tyndale House Ministries, Carol Stream, Illinois 60188. All rights reserved.

Scripture quotations marked NIV are taken from the Holy Bible, New International Version®, NIV®. Copyright © 1973, 1978, 1984, 2011 by Biblica, Inc.™ Used by permission of Zondervan. All rights reserved worldwide. www.zondervan.com The "NIV" and "New International Version" are trademarks registered in the United States Patent and Trademark Office by Biblica, Inc.™

Scripture quotations marked NKJV are taken from the New King James Version®. Copyright © 1982 by Thomas Nelson. Used by permission. All rights reserved.

Scripture quotations marked AMPC are taken from the Amplified® Bible (AMPC), Copyright © 1954, 1958, 1962, 1964, 1965, 1987 by The Lockman Foundation. Used by permission. www. Lockman.org.

Scripture quotations marked GNT are from the Good News Translation in Today's English Version - Second Edition Copyright © 1992 by American Bible Society. Used by Permission.

Scripture quotations marked KJ21 are taken from the 21st Century King James Version®, copyright © 1994. Used by permission of Deuel Enterprises, Inc., Gary, SD 57237. All rights reserved.

Scripture quotations marked GW are taken from the God's Word translation. GOD'S WORD is a copyrighted work of God's Word to the Nations. Quotations are used by permission. Copyright © 1995 by God's Word to the Nations. All rights reserved.

Scriptures marked BLB are taken from The Holy Bible, Berean Literal Bible, BLB Copyright © 2016, 2018 by Bible Hub. Used by Permission. All Rights Reserved Worldwide.

ISBN: 9798568415114

DEDICATION

I dedicate this book to God. From a life of complacency and unrepentant sin, it is only through complete brokenness and God's mercy, grace and forgiveness, that He has brought me to the place of writing books, which I willingly submit to for His purpose and for His glory alone. I am simply His servant, and I delight to do His will, even though at times it is an immense burden to bear.

"Whatever may be your task, work at it heartily (from the soul), as [something done] for the Lord and not for men,

Knowing [with all certainty] that it is from the Lord [and not from men] that you will receive the inheritance which is your [real] reward. [The One Whom] you are actually serving [is] the Lord Christ (the Messiah)." – Colossians 3:23-24 AMPC

ACKNOWLEDGEMENTS

It is with immense gratitude that I offer my thanks to the Reverend Charlynne Boddie for writing the Foreword to this book. Since God brought you into our lives about 5 years ago, your support for the work that both Chris and I have been called by the Lord to do has been immeasurable. May God bless you richly.

I wish to also extend my thanks to three wonderful people who have written endorsements for this book; Olave Snelling, Julie Anderson and Stuart Vickers. I appreciate greatly the time you have all taken out of your own busy schedules to read the manuscript and write such wonderful and encouraging words in support of this work. I pray the Lord brings many blessings into your lives.

Thank you to the team at JWC Creative for using your God-given gift in getting this book published. I lack the ability to turn a manuscript document on my computer into a published work, so your skill in this area is much needed and greatly appreciated. God bless you too!

Finally, I would like to thank all the like-minded brothers and sisters in Christ whom the Lord has brought into my life since 2011 - the year when God decided to wake me up out of my own spiritual slumber. Your encouragement and support with regards to this book, and all the previous books I have written, has kept me anchored to fulfilling what the Lord is compelling me to do.

God bless each and every person who has joined me on this journey.

FOREWORD

As I sit down to write my thoughts about this current offering from the heart of Michele Neal, I cannot help but surmise the timeliness of this particular book of hers. Our world currently finds itself trying to unwind from the aftermath of a global pandemic. Every sector of the planet is reeling from the coronavirus. Most of us have never seen anything like the chaos we are experiencing in our lifetimes.

Many are looking for answers everywhere. Some find themselves looking to the Holy Bible for the first time in their lives. Some people in and outside the Church are asking ministers like myself: "What's it all about? What comes next? Do you believe that the Antichrist is on the way? Are we really in the End Times?"

As an instructor of the Bible and its contents, all things prophetic in particular, I can see that the words of the Bible are coming to pass almost daily at an alarming rate. God's Word is not just a historical book. God's Word is absolute truth. God's Word is the plumb line for everything that pertains to this life and the next. And God Himself tells us that it is impossible for Him to lie about anything. There is no darkness in Him. So, when He speaks of an Antichrist coming on the scene in the End Times, we can trust that it is going to happen.

"For the word of the Lord is right and true; He is faithful in all He does." – Psalm 33:4 NIV

"...God cannot lie when He takes an oath or makes a promise..." – Hebrews 6:18 GW

"This is the message which we have heard from Him and declare to you, that God is light and in Him is no darkness at all." – 1 John 1:5 NIV

"And you will hear of wars and rumours of wars. See that you are not troubled; for all these things must come to pass, but the end is not yet. For nation will rise against nation, and kingdom against kingdom. And there will be famines, pestilences (plagues), and earthquakes in various places... Then many false prophets will rise up and deceive many. And because lawlessness will abound the love of many will grow cold. But he who endures to the end shall be saved."
– Matthew 24:6-7,11-14 NKJV

"Little children, it is the last hour; and as you have heard that the Antichrist is coming, even now many antichrists have come by which we know that it is the last hour...Who is a liar but he who denies that Jesus is the Christ? He is antichrist who denies the Father and the Son." – 1 John 2:18, 22 BLB

Michele has written this book from an honest heart that encourages every person to take the time to read and discover what the Word of God actually tells us about the person who is coming to lead the entire world into total destruction. She encourages us to read and study with eyes, mind and heart wide open.

When I was a pre-teen girl in the 1970s, my youth group leaders and pastors routinely spoke of the coming Kingdom of Jesus Christ and all that would happen here on earth *before* the Rapture and the Second Coming of Christ. I was raised on the whole Word of God and taught that it was right to fear the Lord and Him only. I studied these truths with great excitement and expectation of what it would all be like for those who counted themselves a part of the Bride of Christ. And I pondered in my heart whether or not I would be alive to experience the 'last days'.

"But know this, that in the last days perilous times will come: For men will be lovers of themselves, lovers of money, boasters, proud, blasphemers, disobedient to parents, unthankful, unholy, unloving, unforgiving, slanderers, without self-control, brutal, despisers of good, traitors, headstrong, haughty, lovers of pleasure rather than lovers of God, having a form of godliness but denying its power. And from such people turn away!" – 2 Timothy 3:1-5 NKJV

This book boldly discusses the topics that are rarely talked about in today's world. Where the days of the Church Age are behind us, it is evident that we are fast approaching the Kingdom Age where the Lord begins to prepare His Bride for His Kingdom and His living with us forever. Prepare to be awakened or reminded of foundational truths of our Christian faith as you read the contents of this book.

I believe everything that is happening on planet Earth at this moment in time is preparing the way for the Antichrist and his minions to take center stage and usher in the battle of all battles against every person that God the Father sent His Son to redeem. God promises us that the enemy of our souls will be forever locked up once and for all, but several things must take place before that happens. The Antichrist must rise and carry out his role in fulfilment of all that God foretold. God always tells His children what we can expect in His Word. We must study the Scriptures like never before, to hear and know what He has destined for us all. The enemy's time is almost up, and doesn't he know it! We have God's Word on this truth:

"Therefore rejoice, O heavens, and you who dwell in them! Woe to the inhabitants of the earth and sea! For the devil has come down to you, having great wrath, because he knows that he has a short time." – Revelation 12:12 NLT

Even though our times are challenging, to say the least, I also believe this is the *most* exciting time to be a Christian because His Word *is* coming to pass! Our God is so true to His Word. My questions to anyone who reads this book are: Are you ready? Have you chosen the eternal winning team? Do you wake up every day with peace in your heart because you *know* without a shadow of any doubt where you are going? Do you know how to discern the times in which we live?

Here's what God's Word says:

"Therefore He says: 'Awake, you who sleep, Arise from the dead, And Christ will give you light.' See then that you walk circumspectly, not as fools but wise, redeeming the time, because the days are evil. Therefore do not be unwise, but understand what the will of the Lord is." – Ephesians 5:14-17 NKJV

God's Word is being fulfilled all around us every day. So, let's choose to be alert, super discerning and intimately close to our Lord and His Word in these days. We must listen *and* obey what His still, small voice is saying to us, as we edge ever closer to His appearing.

Blessings to all who choose to read this timely work.

Reverend Charlynne M. Boddie, Managing Director
Charlynne Boddie Ministries
Chichester, West Sussex, UK
September 2020

Minister, International Speaker, TV producer, media consultant and Author of 'No Appointments Necessary' and 'True Grid'. charlynne.com

ENDORSEMENTS

'In the midst of a Covid-19 pandemic, the problems we face individually, nationally and globally are so huge that it is difficult to know where to begin to pray as Christians. But pray we do! One thing is sure. As the writer of 'Antichrist Arising' observes, in the vast increase in incidents that look like something from an apocalyptic movie, we realise that it is not a movie; it is happening in real life now. When two decades ago I was involved in producing a 'Dispatches' programme for Channel 4 about Satanic Ritual Abuse, one 'survivor' who had become a Christian was telling us that when 'the man of lawlessness' put his head above the parapet, we would see horrifically increased levels of lawlessness, chaos, terror and violence worldwide. Well, that man has indeed put his head above the parapet long since and what we see eschatologically is world history heading for the rise of the Antichrist and the eventual return of Christ Himself.

When Michele Neal asked the Lord to speak to her by the power of the Holy Spirit in her usual retreat at the end of the year, little did she realise what He would reveal as she hid herself away to listen. She takes us on a journey through the Scriptures pertaining to the rise of the Antichrist and End Times with a felicitous pared back writing style by which the author links arms with the reader, examining in all humility and earnestly seeking the meaning of the passages. The result is compelling. The Antichrist is arising. The return of the Lord is not too far away. We know these things because we have read the Bible. Let the reader have eyes to see and ears to hear what the Spirit is saying to the churches. These are tumultuous times! This is a terrific book! I commend it wholeheartedly!

My great congratulations to Michele. Writing it was an extraordinary spiritual and literal accomplishment for which, I have no doubt, she and her husband have paid quite a price. What a subject! Nobody could undertake such a task on such an incredible subject without a huge effort and massive anointing and the help 'big time' of the Holy Spirit of God. May Michele's book have great success in penetrating right into the lives of masses of Christians and into the hearts of those who aren't. May it thrive and speak into the spirits of many, many people and turn them towards the soon-coming Jesus.'

— Olave Snelling; Broadcaster, award-winning presenter and producer, documentary maker, media professional, intercessor, former Executive Chairman of the Christian Broadcasting Council.

'LEARN MORE as you read this book about the End Times and what the Bible actually says about the Antichrist arising. This book will challenge how you think truth about life today and what the Bible actually says.'

— Julie Anderson; Senior leader at Commonwealth Christian Fellowship (London); Co-founder of *The Prayer Foundation*, with a call to pray for Parliament and the media; TV Ministry presenter & author of *Rehearsal*.

'This book will challenge how you think about life today and what the Bible says about the Antichrist and the End Times. In my opinion, the author has been insightful, and I love the way Michele has encouraged the reader to dig deeper for themselves by presenting them with different schools of thought on this important End Times subject without just giving her opinion. All in all, a great read. I absolutely loved it.'

— Stuart Vickers; Senior Pastor, Restore Church, Boston, UK

CONTENTS

Then the LORD replied:

"Write down the revelation
and make it plain on tablets
so that a herald may run with it.

For the revelation awaits an appointed time;
it speaks of the end
and will not prove false.

Though it linger, wait for it;
it will certainly come
and will not delay."
– Habakkuk 2:2-3 NIV

"Let no one in any way deceive or entrap you, for that day will not come unless the apostasy comes first [that is, the great rebellion, the abandonment of the faith by professed Christians], and the man of lawlessness is revealed, the son of destruction [the Antichrist, the one who is destined to be destroyed]."

– 2 Thessalonians 2:3 AMP

INTRODUCTION
THE REASON FOR THIS BOOK

"Go into your houses, my people, and shut the door behind you. Hide yourselves for a little while until God's anger is over. The LORD is coming from his heavenly dwelling place to punish the people of the earth for their sins. The murders that were secretly committed on the earth will be revealed, and the ground will no longer hide those who have been killed." – Isaiah 26:20-21 GNT (Author's emphasis)

The opening verse of the passage of scripture above describes all that I am about to share with you.

For the past 10 years, on 31st December of each year, I have taken some specific time to seek the Lord concerning the New Year into which we were heading. December 31st 2019 was no different. I prayed a very simple prayer asking the Lord to reveal to me what He wanted me to know. I sat and waited for a while, and then, with notepad and pen in hand, I wrote down what I felt the Holy Spirit was saying to me. The following are the bullet points of what I felt the Lord impress upon my heart.

1. Take more time out to pray and to read God's Word with diligence, and to worship Him.
2. Pray for the nations, for repentance to come.
3. Live a 'hidden life'.
4. Only go out to buy essentials.

5. Use money more wisely, just for essentials.

I thanked the Lord for giving me what I considered to be a fairly straightforward list of simple disciplines for me to put into practice for 2020, and I did not have any further thoughts about it. But little did I know what was coming…

For most of 2019, I had been feeling a pressure building up within me of something that I could not put my finger on. No matter how much I sought the Lord about this unsettling feeling, He did not give me any response, yet this foreboding feeling began to intensify.

In October 2019, my husband and I moved to a remote, isolated location in Wales, thinking that this sinister feeling would melt away in the silence and solitude of the endless hills and valleys surrounding our home. That was not the case. In fact, the intensity of this feeling increased like a pressure cooker! I spent so much time crying deeply and seeking the Lord day after day, for two months, desperately wanting to find some relief from the burden that was invading my soul.

Throughout this whole time, my husband had also been experiencing this same sensation. It was so consuming that it made us feel extremely tired all the time. No amount of rest or sleep seemed to relieve this overwhelming exhaustion. We sensed that it was probably of spiritual origin, and as no amount of praying alleviated this feeling, we accepted this burden of heaviness as something that the Lord wished us to bear for His purposes. But we still did not know what it was about.

December 31st arrived. No sooner had the fireworks gone off and Big Ben chimed in the New Year of 2020, it seemed that all hell began to be let loose upon the earth. Back to back storms, hurricanes, tornadoes, hail and lightning storms, earthquakes, volcanoes and unprecedented floods raged across the nations of the world. Then came reports of plagues of locusts swarming from country to country, with reports that the size of the swarms were multiplying, as well as the physical size of the locusts, up to the size of a person's forearm!

Added to this, reports of birds falling from the sky in great numbers, and sea creatures washed up on the shores in various locations around the world. All of this being hot on the heels of relentless wildfires ravaging the earth, leaving towns and villages looking like scenes from an apocalyptic movie… only this was *not* a movie, and it is happening in real life, right now.

Many will say that these things have been happening now and again throughout the centuries. This is true, but these events have been increasing over the past 10 years to the point that they are now converging all at the same time. It seems there is no let-up in catastrophic events bombarding the earth, and no sooner has one thing subsided, another disaster takes its place. There seems to be no rest and no peace for humanity, and many 'experts' tell us that what we are experiencing will be something we will have to get used to, referring to it as 'the new normal'.

With all that I was seeing on the daily news, I began to reflect on the list that the Lord gave to me on 31st December 2019. It made sense that I should be praying more fervently for the nations, asking God to reveal to each government the sins which they were condoning and legalizing to appease the voices of politically correct and persuasive minority-interest lobby groups; asking God to bring them all to repentance for implementing laws that legalized sin. One of those laws is the gruesome abortion of unborn babies in the womb now being allowed in various countries right up to the moment of birth, and any babies that survive abortion being either left to die on the abortion table, or killed by the abortionist. As if this is not evil enough, I recently read that 94% of physicians in Belgium support what is called 'after birth abortions'. This is the killing of babies *after* they have been born if they have any disabilities; not only for serious, life-threatening disabilities, but also for non-lethal conditions such as Down Syndrome, cleft lip and club foot. It goes even further than this; these people support killing babies who are simply not wanted…*after* they have been born.

Something that, only a decade ago, would have hardly entered anyone's thinking, is now being deemed as something that should be accepted by society, and promoted as a woman's human right to do.

For more information on this, visit https://righttolife.org. uk/news/94-of-belgian-doctors-surveyed-support-after-birth-abortion-for-babies-with-disabilities/

I mention this particular sin of the nations because of a specific part of what is written in the scripture passage at the head of this Introduction;

> "The murders that were secretly committed on the
> earth will be revealed, and the ground will no longer
> hide those who have been killed."

The shedding of innocent blood is so serious to God. When we read the whole of the scripture passage at the head of this Introduction; it is clear that the committing of this sin is going to bring His wrath upon the earth.

As I was reflecting on the list of points that God gave to me and putting into practice the need for praying for the nations to repent, I couldn't understand why, for 2020, He was instructing me to *live a hidden life*. What was I supposed to shut myself indoors for, and why was God telling me to *only go out to buy essentials*? This seemed somewhat strange to me as we live in a nation that has traditionally had no restrictions to daily life, and is blessed with an abundance of food and other possessions for every comfort of modern living. Maybe God was just instructing me to be a bit more mindful about the difference between what I wanted, compared to what I actually needed. This seemed a fairly reasonable conclusion, and I decided that I would make diligent efforts to put this into effect. But it turned out that God's words to me on December 31st 2019 were in fact a warning that meant I would *not* be the only one living a hidden life and only going out to buy essentials…

Global Lockdown

As January 2020 unfolded, 'Breaking News' flashed onto our TV screens. A pestilence had been unleashed on the world, affecting a great many nations and sending them into panic and lockdown; the pestilence of a coronavirus known as Covid19. As I write this introduction at the start of April 2020, the virus has swept the globe, and nations' economies are grinding to a halt. People who we know, and even family members, have been affected by it. In the effort to save people's lives, world governments have imposed a strict lockdown on their citizens, ordering businesses, shops, eating establishments, schools, churches and other places of worship, and commerce of every kind (except *essential* services) to close for the foreseeable future. In effect, the world has been ordered to 'stay at home'. Many nations have imposed travel restrictions, only allowing people to drive a few miles for their *essentials*. Over-zealous police forces are using high-tech drones to search out people who are not adhering to government 'guidelines' and are also imposing hefty fines for non-compliance.

Medical Centres are closed to their patients. Consultations are by telephone only. Hospitals have gone into overdrive, including the rapid building of huge temporary hospitals, in preparation for what they believe will be a deluge of sick people all needing intensive care.

Many Accident and Emergency departments, usually overflowing with patients, have become almost empty due to the UK Government ordering us not to overload our emergency services for the foreseeable future. This has put at risk the lives of very many people with *non*-Covid19 illnesses, potentially leading to their death because they have felt unable to access any health care or treatment.

Many national leaders are urging the public not to use cash

when making purchases, stating that money changing hands could transfer the virus. We are told to only make payments with debit or credit cards.

When I heard our Prime Minister, Boris Johnson, say the words *'stay at home'* and *'only go out to buy essentials'*, alarm bells went off in my soul and my whole body felt shaken to the core. What the Prime Minister had said were words that were almost identical to God's words to me on New Year's Eve 2019 in relation to 2020, to *'live a hidden life'* (in effect, 'stay at home') and *'only go out to buy essentials'*. The shock and reality of this absolutely thundered through my being. My eyes opened wide and my jaw dropped to the floor in utter astonishment! It dawned on me that what I thought was a very simple instruction from the Lord to be more mindful in how I live on a daily basis, was in fact a revelation concerning what was about to come upon the whole of the earth; the almost total shutdown of the normal way of life we have all known since the 1960s.

A fast sweeping viral pandemic has caused much of the world to come to a grinding halt. The fear of citizens being infected by the Covid19 virus, and the fear of death is what has caused national leaders to take the drastic, crippling actions of shutting down most of normal life. There is a push to have a 'temporary' global government to supposedly oversee the world's management during the pandemic, and in view of the economies of most countries plummeting into the depths, there is now talk of bringing in a global digital currency. As with most temporary arrangements, these usually end up becoming permanent, under the guise of being 'for the greater good'.

These reactions to a viral outbreak are unprecedented. If they have now succeeded in locking down most of life, and containing us in our homes indefinitely, with further threats of a future 'second wave' occurring if we slacken off in our vigilance, what measures will they take to restrain and contain us if a second wave does come, or even another 'new' virus? Is this global response a sign of things to come? Are all these events, and the responses to them, a gradual build up to what is prophesied in the Bible concerning the End Times, a cashless society giving rise to a global digital currency, a New World Order with a global leader, the appearing of the Antichrist, a One World Religion, and the implementation of the Mark of the Beast, without which we will not be able to buy or sell anything? To fulfil this prophecy, it would seem that a disturbing event would have to trigger a sudden change in the way the world is run; an event that has the whole world so fearful, people will do anything that their leaders require of them so that they can return to normal life. They will hail and honour anyone who will declare that they have got the solution to the global dilemma.

Some of our Christian friends and acquaintances, who we spoke to during 2019, also shared our feeling that something big was about to happen on the earth, at some point. They also couldn't verbalize what it was. They just felt a sense of deep foreboding in their spirit. None of us could have foreseen what has now gripped the earth and brought it to a crushing standstill in what seems like a split second of time.

We have noticed that God has been gradually shaking the nations over the years in an attempt to get their attention, but it seems that, despite any destruction that befalls each country, their leaders stand up and defiantly declare that they will rebuild from the ruins. They seem to take no time to reflect on why such carnage has fallen on their nation, and they carry on regardless, implementing and legalizing wickedness to their heart's content, when in fact they ought to be on their knees before God in confession and repentance of the sins of their nation, seeking His forgiveness, and rebuilding their nations based on obedience to His Word.

The Sound of Silence

Instead of rising up to preach God's Word concerning

the increasing catastrophes occurring all over the globe, the institutional church has largely remained silent. Its leaders seem to cower in a corner, not wanting to speak to the nations' leaders like the prophets and apostles in the Bible did when they confronted the nations about the stench of their sins in the sight of God. All we see is archbishops and other senior church leaders offering peaceful platitudes to comfort the people, lighting candles and asking God to heal the pain of the people's suffering. National suffering is usually caused by immense national sin; a departing from the ways of God throughout every area of society. The only way that this level of suffering can be relieved, and the land healed, is through our national church leaders calling our nations' leaders and its citizens to confess and repent of its collective and individual sin and wickedness.

But the corridors of church hierarchy around the world remain deafeningly silent on this matter of such national importance. The Church itself is neck-deep in many of its own unrepentant sins, yet overriding all of these, it is drowning in the sins of serious negligence and dereliction of its God-ordained duty to guide and lead the nations in the ways of the Lord. The institutional church has become a liberal, politically correct organisation, simply to please the State and to do what the nations' leaders want it to.

When church leaders abandon their role as God's watchmen over the nations, failing to instruct the leaders to implement and uphold godly, righteous laws, then the nations will gradually cast aside historical Christian laws and allow sin to be made legal, and label this as 'freedom' and 'progress'.

God sees all of this, and He is not pleased. The world is saturated in sin and all manner of evil. Having refused to heed God's warnings, it would now appear that He is shaking the nations all at the same time. It is so sudden and so violent that all of humanity seems to be reeling with the shock that life as we have always known it has changed in an instant, and it may never be the same again. It is an event which has much foreboding, with many looking for answers to questions that their national leaders cannot give them. These leaders are looking to appoint one *global leader* to solve all of the world's problems, and every effort will be made to ensure this happens, under the guise of world peace and safety.

Conspiracy Theories

Many believe that what is happening is political; politics may be involved in the visible signs that we are seeing, but ultimately what is happening is *biblical*...the unfolding of End Times Bible prophecy. Yet many people, including Christians, dismissively and even mockingly label any discussion on what is happening as merely a 'conspiracy theory'. I am deeply concerned that many believers do not seem to want to consider what it would take to usher in these huge prophetic End Times events upon the world. To go from our everyday normal life to sudden global control, something needs to happen that will bring immense fear, so that a world leader can arise who will bring in a global 'solution'.

Let's use a biblical example from Genesis chapters 6-8: In the time of Noah, because all of humanity was corrupt and full of violence, God told Noah that He was going to put an end to all the people and the earth with a great flood. God told Noah to build a colossal ark in order to save himself and his family, along with a male and female of every living creature. Meanwhile, the people carried on living their lives as if nothing was ever going to happen, no doubt mocking and laughing at Noah for the enormous ark he was building. The Bible doesn't actually give any account as to whether Noah warned the people of what was coming, but as they would have seen what he was building, it is highly likely they would have questioned him as to why he was building it, and we could assume that he would have answered them. One could imagine the people labelling Noah as a conspiracy theorist with his message of doom! Noah was around 500 years old when he began building the ark. For 100 years the people witnessed this but failed to heed the warning that the building of this ark meant. When Noah was 600 years old, God sent the flood as prophesied and the whole of the human race perished, except for Noah and his family and the animals in the ark.

This example is not just a story to tell our children. It is a warning in the Bible for us to take to heart and learn from. Many of us feel the need to limit the workings and the ways of God to fit our small, finite minds. We think that, in order for something to be 'of God', what He does must fall within our human capacity of understanding. Our natural minds struggle to accept that God may do things in very strange ways to bring to fulfilment the things that are prophesied in His Word. If something seems too far-fetched, we feel that it cannot possibly be 'of God'. But we forget that God's ways and thoughts are higher than ours (see Isaiah 55:8-9).

If the Lord can use a 500-600 year old man to build a humungous ark, and cause a cataclysmic flood to destroy the world, and in the time of Moses, bring devastating plagues (the water turning to blood, the frogs, the lice, the flies, the livestock pestilence, the boils, the hail, the thunder and fire, the plague of locusts, and finally the smiting of all the first-born in Egypt), upon a nation and its leader who *persistently* mocked God and held God's people captive; why do we think that God would *not* use such strange and even bizarre measures in the 21st century to bring about the fulfilment of His Word concerning End Times events and the rise of the Antichrist?

There is only one being who wants us to think this. It is Satan. He wants to keep us in ignorance of what is coming upon the earth. He doesn't want us to investigate anything that might alert us to the Antichrist's agenda being worked out through his human minions on earth.

The Antichrist spirit

If we assume that, say, two-thirds of the global population are not followers of Christ, then being non-believers, they are followers of beliefs and religions that are anti-Christian. Any belief system that is *anti-Christian* is following a leader or a deity that is of the Antichrist. Every person who is not a Christian is someone whom Satan can use to fulfil his plans on the earth.

If the government of a nation has only a handful of members who are Christians, the rest of the members of that government either believe in or are following something or someone else. Those who are not *for* Christ are *against* Christ (see Matthew 12:30); therefore, they are of the Antichrist.

Drawing this to its logical conclusion, any government that is made up of a large majority of people who *do not* wish to follow Christ will push for policies and laws that reflect their anti-Christian agendas. The Antichrist's agenda ultimately is global control, world domination, a New World Order with a One World Religion, and a global currency which, in order to be used, will require every person to accept the 'Mark of the Beast' on the right hand or the forehead (see Revelation 13:16). We need to snap out of our complacency and realise that *something* has got to bring this about, and it may not sit comfortably with our human way of thinking, simply because we want to preserve our comfortable way of life.

God has prophesied what is coming upon the earth in the End Times, and He is warning us, in the strongest possible terms, to wake up or we will be overwhelmed by the unspeakable events. This is *not* a conspiracy theory...it is a Biblical truth that will be fulfilled at the appointed time. God is warning us for our ultimate good...if we will humble ourselves before Him and pay attention.

As we begin to get into the meat of this book, I want to point out to you, right from the start, that I am not a theologian. I would say that I am in the same category as the first disciples, who were ordinary people with no special training in the scriptures (see Acts 4:13), but they were able to speak the Word of God boldly because they had been with Jesus and had been filled with the Holy Spirit. Their lack of training in God's Word did not prevent God from using them to speak with His authority to all those around them. The Apostle John was one of Jesus' first disciples; he was a fisherman, and yet Jesus gave John the vision of the End Times, which he faithfully recorded for us in detail in the Book of Revelation.

The purpose of this book is to look at events that are occurring on the earth in order to discern if what we are seeing and hearing lines up with God's Word. I want to take the contents of this Introduction and provide you with answers from scripture, to what is happening from God's perspective. If the Lord is shaking the nations, then His Word will show us what is going on and what it is all leading to… the rise of the Antichrist.

So, let us begin this journey. Despite the difficult things that we will encounter, in the midst of it all there is great joy for those who are followers of Christ. At the end of the book, all who do not yet know Jesus Christ as their Lord and Saviour will be encouraged to make the choice that will change the course of their eternal destiny. I am praying for you.

Chapter 1

THE ANTICHRIST –
A REAL PERSON, OR A FAIRY TALE?

"How you are fallen from heaven,
O Lucifer, son of the morning!
How you are cut down to the ground,
You who weakened the nations!
 For you have said in your heart:
…I will exalt my throne above the stars of God…"
– Isaiah 14:12-13(a) NKJV

What does the word 'Antichrist' mean? It means someone who is *against* Christ. In reality, anyone who rejects Jesus Christ and His message of salvation through faith in Him, is effectively anti-Christian, and thereby is 'anti-Christ' in their personal beliefs and opinions.

Is there really a being or a person known as the Antichrist? If there is, why should we be concerned about something that many believe is just a fairy tale?

When we were children, we may have read stories of good and evil, with demons and devils playing their part in the narrative. Some of these stories may have given us nightmares, and we found ourselves unable to sleep peacefully unless we had a night-light on in our bedroom! But as we grew up, we tended to put away these stories and thought no more about such things.

However, God's Word, the Holy Bible, from start to finish, is full of accounts of the devil, Satan, the serpent, the beast, and the Antichrist. So, we really ought to pay attention to what God has to say about this evil entity, and why such a being exists.

Let's start at the very beginning. I will give a simplified account.

Before God created the human race, heaven was full of holy angelic beings, one of these being Lucifer. At the head of this chapter, the Bible passage tells us that he was known as the son of the morning. He would have walked and talked and communed with God, in the same way as every other holy angelic being in heaven. Whatever God desired to do, He would have appointed His angels to carry out tasks in order to undertake His work.

In Genesis chapter 3, after God had created the earth and all that is in it, He then saw that the earth needed taking care of, and so God created the first human beings. He created them male and female, and these first humans were Adam and Eve.

God created Adam and Eve in His own likeness, which would have been in absolute perfection, and they communed with God on the earth in a place called the Garden of Eden. They had access to all that they could possibly want in order to enjoy their life in God's perfect creation. But God gave them just one commandment to obey; they were commanded to not eat the fruit of the tree of the knowledge of good and evil. They knew only how to do what was good and right and pleasing to God, so if they ate this 'forbidden fruit' they would gain the knowledge of evil, which would utterly destroy their created perfection, and would result in them no longer being able to remain in the presence of God.

Having seen that God created human beings in His own perfect image, with no sin or evil in them at the time of their creation, and knowing that God created this perfect human race to share in the joy of living in His presence for eternity, the angelic being Lucifer became jealous of what God had created. Lucifer, full of pride, rebelled against God, and as the passage at the head of this chapter tells us, he was thrown out of heaven and down to the earth.

Following his rebellion and his eviction from heaven, Lucifer, no longer the son of the morning, now becomes the devil or Satan. He appears in the Garden of Eden as a serpent, with evil intent. Having rebelled against God, and having lost his place in heaven, his plan was to tempt these perfect human beings to also rebel against God and thereby lose their place in God's presence too. He slithers up to Eve and, using God's command to them to not eat the fruit of the tree of the knowledge of good and evil, he twists God's Word just enough to cause Eve to doubt in her mind, by questioning her, *"Did God really say…?"* (See Genesis 3:1).

Satan knew that the moment he could get Adam and Eve to doubt God's Word, they would succumb to the temptation and eat the forbidden fruit, and would gain the knowledge of evil. Satan knew that once they became aware of what evil was, God would banish them from His presence for eternity. Because Satan will never enter heaven ever again, he decided on a mission which would stop the entire human race from entering heaven. His plan succeeded the moment that Eve believed his lie and ate the fruit. She then handed it to Adam, and he ate of it. That very act of rebellion caused their eyes to be opened to sin and evil, and they were so ashamed, they hid themselves from God.

God banished them from the Garden of Eden (paradise) and posted cherubim with a flaming sword to guard the way to the tree of life.

Since that time, all human beings have been born with the inherent disposition of sin in our DNA, and as such, by this very fact, and through no personal fault of our own, we are all *outside* of the presence of God. Without being aware of it, we are all born into this world needing a Saviour to save our soul from the eternal penalty and punishment of our inherent disposition of sin. Because we are born with this terminal condition of sin, every single one of us needs to be saved from sin's eternal outcome. Satan knows this, and his mission is to do everything he can to prevent us from finding out how to be saved. Satan wants as many of us as possible to stay in our sin and remain in his kingdom of darkness. He does not want anyone to find out how to enter the kingdom of Light and be saved from the eternal consequences of sin.

As God created the human race for His purposes and for His glory, and to dwell with Him forever, with all humanity now being outside His kingdom due to our inherent sin from the rebellion of Adam and Eve, God had to do something to bring His salvation to us. In due time, God sent His Son Jesus Christ into the world to be our Saviour, to save us from our sins. Jesus preached that we must repent and be born again to enter the kingdom of heaven. He showed us by His own example the need for baptism, and He told us that we can be filled with the Holy Spirit in the same way as the first disciples on the day of Pentecost. He taught that those who obey His Word are His followers (see John 8:31 NLT). Believing, following and having faith in Christ will bring us salvation, transferring us from Satan's kingdom of darkness and into God's kingdom of Light. This is a gift from God. No works on our own part can bring about our salvation. All of this is what Satan does not want anyone to discover, and he will unleash his hordes of demons to come against anyone who may be in reach of salvation.

From the time of the creation of the human race, Satan has been relentless in his evil scheming to thwart the salvation of all who desire to turn to Jesus Christ in faith. Satan's demons are the fallen angels that were cast down with him (see Isaiah 14:12-15), and like a despot leader with his wicked army, he will order them to blockade every path we take, and hurl their fiery darts at us in their attempt to destroy any faith that we may have. The simple fact is, God is not going to allow Satan and his demons to enter into heaven. As a result, Satan will unleash all the forces of hell in his attempt to stop us getting their too.

His assaults on humanity will continue until the day of Christ's Second Coming. But until that time, the Bible tells us that, the closer we get to that glorious day, things on earth will grow increasingly more evil, coupled with many signs in the heavens and on the earth, which will lead to the rise of the Antichrist, a man who will be invaded by Satan himself. He will initially appear as the 'saviour' of a desperate world that is crying out for someone to fix the world's problems and deliver them from the chaos. This man will do this, and, for a period of time everyone will hail him and worship him. But at a certain point, he will change very suddenly, and show his true colours. This man who 'saves the world' will become the satanic embodiment of the Antichrist.

We will look at the End Times signs and the visible appearing of the Antichrist in later chapters. But for now, we will move on to the next chapter to look at how the Antichrist is mentioned in Bible prophecy in the Old Testament book of Daniel.

Chapter 2

THE ANTICHRIST –
ACCORDING TO THE BOOK OF DANIEL

We saw in Chapter 1 that Lucifer, one of God's angels rebelled against God and was thrown out of heaven and down to the earth. In the Book of Genesis, we know that the fallen angel Lucifer is Satan, the serpent. We will see in this chapter, and throughout this book, that Satan will give his power to the person who will become the End Times Antichrist.

Most prophecies given in the Old Testament were specific to those actual times and concerned the people to whom the prophet was speaking. However, there are also many prophecies that clearly did not relate to the times they were living in. These were prophecies relating to the future, often shown in dreams and visions, and concerned the times of the end. These End Times prophecies, recorded by the Old Testament prophets, were intended by the Lord to be recognized and understood only by those who would become the generation that will *"not pass away until all these things have happened"* (see Matthew 24:34). In recent years, Old Testament prophecies have been, and are being fulfilled at a phenomenal rate. Sadly, so much that is of a biblical nature is not reported in the mainstream news. But with round-the-clock instant access to reports on social media, we can easily find out what is happening, although we should use discernment and wisdom to check that information that is shared is not 'fake news'.

In this chapter we will look at what many Bible scholars view as the most important Book in the Old Testament concerning the End Times; the Book of Daniel. Around the year 553 BC, the archangel Gabriel gave Daniel a vision of the future, and we know that this relates to the End Times because what is revealed to him is in line with what Jesus tells His disciples in the Gospels, and what the angel of the Lord also shows to the Apostle John in the Book of Revelation. We will look at both of these in Chapters 3 and 6 respectively.

Another reason we know that the vision Daniel was given relates to the End Times is because twice the archangel instructed him to seal up the prophetic visions that he was shown *"until the time of the end"* (see Daniel 12:4) and *"until the appointed time of the end"* (see Daniel 8:19). This would seem to indicate that at the time of the end, both the meaning and the fulfilment of these End Times prophecies would become unsealed and made available for discernment to the generation that will *"not pass away until all these things have happened"* (see Luke 21:32).

When we look at the Book of Revelation later on, we will see that the angel of the Lord gave John the visions of the End Times which confirm those given by the archangel Gabriel to Daniel. In John's angelic encounter around 95 AD, after showing him all the visions of the future, the angel of the Lord instructed him *"**not to seal up** the words of the prophecy of this book, for the time is near"* (see Revelation 22:10 –Author's emphasis).

If Daniel's prophetic visions were sealed until the appointed time of the end, and around 648 years later, John was told not to seal up the prophecy that he was given, if both Daniel's and John's visions relate to the time of the end, then, as the prophetic visions given to John were given hundreds of years after those given to Daniel, we must conclude that these End Times prophecies are *no longer sealed* and have in fact been open since the time of John's vision, and have been gradually unfolding since that time. If this is the case, then it appears that all that remains is for their complete fulfilment. This should be a very sobering thought to anyone who professes to be a believer.

Could we be the final generation that Jesus referred to in Matthew 24:34; the generation that will see all the End Times events coming to pass? Up until the invention of the computer and the rapid progression into other areas of technology over the past few decades, it was not possible to collect the vast amounts of information that is now readily available relating to world events. Now we can share information around the globe at the touch of a few buttons. No period in history has had this ability.

So, let's enter into the vision given to the prophet Daniel and see what is shown to him. The visions refer to beasts, rams, goats, heads, and horns. It is easy to become confused as to what it all means. However, many Bible scholars believe this refers to kingdoms, nations, leaders of nations, political alliances, and a religious organization that would appear to represent Christianity but is in fact a deception. We will examine these details later in the book, but for now we will look at the scriptures relating to the vision given to Daniel, in particular the arrival of the one who will become the Antichrist. In this vision, the Antichrist appears at the point in Daniel chapter 7 that I have emphasized in bold on the next page. Further on in that same chapter, where the archangel Gabriel gives Daniel the interpretation of the dream, I have also highlighted in bold the part that refers to the End Times global regime which will be led by the Antichrist.

As Daniel's visions are confirmed by Jesus in the Book of Revelation, we can be sure that what was revealed to him will come to pass upon the earth at the appointed time of the end. God says that His Word does not return to Him void and that it will accomplish His purpose (see Isaiah 55:11).

Daniel's Dream of Four Beasts

Daniel 7:1-28 AMP

'In the first year of Belshazzar king of Babylon Daniel had a dream and visions appeared in his mind as he lay on his bed; then he wrote the dream down and related a summary of it. Daniel said, "I saw in my vision by night, and behold, the four winds of heaven were stirring up the great sea (the nations). And four great beasts, each different from the other, were coming up out of the sea [in succession]. The first (the Babylonian Empire under Nebuchadnezzar) was like a lion and had the wings of an eagle. I kept looking until its wings were plucked, and it was lifted up from the ground and made to stand on two feet like a man; a human mind was given to it. And behold, another beast, a second one (the Medo-Persian Empire), was like a bear, and it was raised up on one side (domain), and three ribs were in its mouth between its teeth; and it was told, 'Arise, devour much meat.' After this I kept looking, and behold, another one (the Greek Empire of Alexander the Great), like a leopard, which had on its back four wings like those of a bird; the beast also had four heads (Alexander's generals, his successors), and power to rule was given to it. After this I kept looking in the night visions, and behold, [I saw] a fourth beast (the Roman Empire), terrible and extremely strong; and it had huge iron teeth. It devoured and crushed and trampled down what was left with its feet. It was different from all the beasts that came before it, and it had ten horns (ten kings). **While I was considering the horns, behold, there came up among them another horn, a little one, and three of the first horns were pulled up by the roots before it; and behold, in this horn were eyes like the eyes of a man and a mouth boasting of great things.**

The Ancient of Days Reigns

"I kept looking
Until thrones were set up,
And the Ancient of Days (God) took His seat;
His garment was white as snow
And the hair of His head like pure wool.
His throne was flames of fire;
Its wheels were a burning fire.

"A river of fire was flowing
And coming out from before Him;
A thousand thousands were attending Him,
And ten thousand times ten thousand were
standing before Him;
The court was seated,
And the books were opened.

Then I kept looking because of the sound of the great
and boastful words which the horn was speaking. I kept
looking until the beast was slain, and its body destroyed
and given to be burned with fire. As for the rest of the
beasts, their power was taken away; yet their lives were
prolonged [for the length of their lives was fixed] for a
predetermined time.

The Son of Man Presented

"I kept looking in the night visions,
And behold, on the clouds of heaven
One like a Son of Man was coming,
And He came up to the Ancient of Days
And was presented before Him.

"And to Him (the Messiah) was given dominion
(supreme authority),
Glory and a kingdom,
That all the peoples, nations, and speakers of every

language
Should serve and worship Him.
His dominion is an everlasting dominion
Which will not pass away;
And His kingdom is one
Which will not be destroyed.

The Vision Interpreted

"As for me, Daniel, my spirit was distressed and anxious within me, and the visions [that appeared] in my mind kept alarming (agitating) me. I approached one of those who stood by and began asking him the exact meaning of all this. So he told me and explained to me the interpretation of the things: 'These four great beasts are four kings who will arise from the earth. But the saints (believers) of the Most High [God] will receive the kingdom and possess the kingdom forever, for all ages to come.'

"Then I wished to know the exact meaning of the fourth beast, which was different from all the others, extremely dreadful, with teeth of iron and claws of bronze, which devoured, crushed and trampled down what was left with its feet, and the meaning of the ten horns (kings) that were on its head and the other horn which came up later, and before which three of the horns fell, specifically, that horn which had eyes and a mouth that boasted great things and which looked larger than the others. As I kept looking, that horn was making war with the saints (believers) and overpowering them until the Ancient of Days came and judgment was passed in favor of the saints of the Most High [God], and the time arrived when the saints (believers) took possession of the kingdom.

"Thus the angel said, 'The fourth beast shall be a fourth kingdom on earth, which will be different from all other kingdoms and will devour the whole earth and tread it down, and crush it. **As for the ten horns, out of this kingdom ten kings will arise; and another will arise after them, and he will be different from the former ones, and he will subdue three kings. He will speak words against the Most High [God] and wear down the saints of the Most High, and he will intend to change the times and the law; and they will be given into his hand for a time, [two] times, and half a time [three and one-half years].** But the court [of the Most High] will sit in judgment, and his dominion will be taken away, [first to be] consumed [gradually] and [then] to be destroyed forever. Then the kingdom and the dominion and the greatness of all the kingdoms under the whole heaven will be given to the people of the saints (believers) of the Most High; His kingdom will be an everlasting kingdom, and all the dominions will serve and obey Him.'

"This is the end of the matter. As for me, Daniel, my [waking] thoughts were extremely troubling and alarming and my face grew pale; but I kept the matter [of the vision and the angel's explanation] to myself." (Author's emphasis)

We can see that, at the time of the end, an alliance of ten nations (kingdoms) will be in control of the world, headed up by a powerful leader (the little horn that pushes up and removes three of the other leaders) who will be the Antichrist. He will speak against God and oppress His holy people and will try to change the set times and laws. By this we can assume that he will try to change or do away with long-established Judeo-Christian teaching, laws and holy festivals.

This is happening now in many nations which have been founded on Christianity. But when this world approaches the time of the 3½ years midway point of the 7-year Great Tribulation (referred to in the above passage as 'a time, times and half a time'),

Judeo-Christian persecution will intensify exponentially.

As Daniel's vision relates to the time of the Antichrist during his global rule in the Great Tribulation, the holy people mentioned in this passage are the Tribulation saints (both Gentile and Jewish); those who come to faith in Christ during the Great Tribulation, who listened to the Two Witnesses in Revelation 11 (which we will look at later, in Chapter 6). These are the saints that the Antichrist wages war against.

Later in this book I will show this to be the case because we will see that all those who come to faith in Christ *before* the Great Tribulation will no longer be on the earth, because Jesus will come for them, rapturing them out of this world before God pours out His wrath upon the world of unbelievers and the unrepentant.

The Antichrist rises to power during the Great Tribulation. His purpose is to control all who have refused to believe in Jesus Christ. By the very fact that they have rejected Christ, they belong to Satan. They are now his, for him to do with them whatever evil desire he wishes. But his demonic rule will not last long, and his power will be destroyed forever.

Next, in Daniel chapter 8, the archangel gives him further explanation of the vision which he received in Daniel chapter 7, and so I won't add any of my own comments afterwards.

Daniel 8: 1-27 – AMP

Vision of the Ram and Goat

"In the third year of the reign of King Belshazzar a [second] vision appeared to me, Daniel, [this was two years] after the one that first appeared to me. I looked in the vision and it seemed that I was at the citadel of Susa, [the capital of Persia], which is in the province of Elam; and I looked in the vision and I saw myself by the Ulai Canal. Then I raised my eyes and looked, and behold, there in front of the canal stood a [lone] ram (the Medo-Persian Empire) which had two horns. The two horns were high, but one (Persia) was higher than the other (Media), and the higher one came up last. I saw the ram (Medo-Persia) charging westward and northward and southward; no beast could stand before him, nor was there anyone who could rescue [anything] from his power, but he did as he pleased and magnified himself.

"As I was observing [this], behold, a male goat (Greece) was coming from the west [rushing] across the face of the whole earth without touching the ground; and the goat had a conspicuous and remarkable horn (Alexander the Great) between his eyes. He came up to the ram that had the two horns, which I had seen standing in front of the canal, and charged at him in [the fury of] his power and wrath. [In my vision] I saw him come close to the ram (Medo-Persia), and he was filled with rage toward him; and the goat (Greece) struck the ram and shattered his two horns, and the ram had no strength to stand before him. So the goat threw him to the ground and trampled on him, and there was no one who could rescue the ram from his power. Then the male goat magnified himself exceedingly, and when he was [young and] strong, the great horn (Alexander) was [suddenly] broken; and in its place there came up four prominent horns [among whom the kingdom was divided, one] toward [each of] the four winds of heaven.

The Little Horn

"Out of one of them (Antiochus IV Epiphanes) came forth a rather small horn [but one of irreverent presumption and profane pride] which grew exceedingly powerful toward the south, toward the east, and toward the Beautiful Land (Israel). And [in my vision] this horn grew up to the host of heaven, and caused some of the host and some of the stars to fall to the earth, and it trampled on them. Indeed, it magnified itself to be equal with the Commander of the host [of heaven]; and it took away from Him the daily sacrifice (burnt offering), and the place of His sanctuary was thrown down (profaned). Because of the transgression [of God's people—their irreverence and ungodliness] the host will be given over to the wicked horn, along with the regular sacrifice; and righteousness and truth will be flung to the ground, and the horn will do as it pleases [by divine permission] and prosper. Then I heard a holy one (angel) speaking, and another holy one said to the one who was speaking, "How much time will be required to complete the vision regarding the regular sacrifice, the transgression that brings horror, and the trampling underfoot of both the sanctuary and the host [of the people]?" He said to me, "For 2,300 evenings and mornings; then the sanctuary will be cleansed and properly restored."

Interpretation of the Vision

"When I, Daniel, had seen the vision, I sought to understand it; then behold, standing before me was one who looked like a man. And I heard the voice of a man between the banks of the Ulai, which called out and said, "Gabriel, give this man (Daniel) an understanding of the vision." So he came near where I was standing, and when he came I was frightened and fell face downward; but he said to me, "Understand, son of man, that the [**fulfillment of the**] **vision pertains to** [**events that will occur in**] **the time of the end.**"

"Now as he (Gabriel) was speaking with me, I drifted into a deep sleep (unconsciousness) with my face to the ground; but he touched me and made me stand [where

I had stood before]. He said, **"Behold, I am going to let you know what will happen during the final time of the indignation and wrath [of God upon the ungodly], for it concerns the appointed time of the end.**

The Ram's Identity

"The ram which you saw with the two horns represents the kings of Media and Persia.

The Goat

"The shaggy (rough-coated) male goat represents the kingdom of Greece, and the great horn between his eyes is the first king. Regarding the shattered horn and the four others that arose in its place, four kingdoms will rise from his (Alexander's) nation, although not with his power and heritage.

"At the latter period of their reign,
When the transgressors have finished,
A king will arise
Insolent and skilled in intrigue and cunning.

"His power will be mighty, but not by his own power;
And he will corrupt and destroy in an astonishing manner
And [he will] prosper and do exactly as he wills;
He shall corrupt and destroy mighty men and the holy people.

"And through his shrewdness
He will cause deceit to succeed by his hand (influence);
He will magnify himself in his mind,
He will corrupt and destroy many who enjoy a false sense of security.
He will also stand up and oppose the Prince of princes,

But he will be broken, and that by no human hand
[but by the hand of God].

"The vision of the evenings and the mornings
Which has been told [to you] is true.
**But keep the vision a secret,
For it has to do with many days in the now distant
future."**

"And I, Daniel, was exhausted and was sick for [several]
days. Afterward I got up and continued with the king's
business; but I was astounded at the vision, and there was
no one who could explain it." (Author's emphasis)

Now we will look at what is known as 'Daniel's Seventy Weeks';
a prophetic timeline given to him by the archangel Gabriel. Let's
read the passage and then I will comment on it afterwards.

Daniel 9:20-27 AMP

Gabriel Brings an Answer

"While I was still speaking and praying, and confessing
my sin and the sin of my people Israel, and presenting
my supplication before the LORD my God in behalf of
the holy mountain of my God, while I was still speaking
in prayer and extremely exhausted, the man Gabriel,
whom I had seen in the earlier vision, came to me about
the time of the evening sacrifice. He instructed me and
he talked with me and said, "O Daniel, I have now come
to give you insight and wisdom and understanding. At
the beginning of your supplications, the command [to
give you an answer] was issued, and I have come to tell
you, for you are highly regarded and greatly beloved.
Therefore consider the message and begin to understand
the [meaning of the] vision.

Seventy Weeks and the Messiah

"Seventy weeks [of years, or 490 years] have been decreed for your people and for your holy city (Jerusalem), to finish the transgression, to make an end of sins, to make atonement (reconciliation) for wickedness, to bring in everlasting righteousness (right-standing with God), to seal up vision and prophecy and prophet, and to anoint the Most Holy Place. So you are to know and understand that from the issuance of the command to restore and rebuild Jerusalem until [the coming of] the Messiah (the Anointed One), the Prince, there will be seven weeks [of years] and sixty-two weeks [of years]; it will be built again, with [a city] plaza and moat, even in times of trouble. Then after the sixty-two weeks [of years] the Anointed One will be cut off [and denied His Messianic kingdom] and have nothing [and no one to defend Him], and the people of the [other] prince who is to come will destroy the city and the sanctuary. Its end will come with a flood; even to the end there will be war; desolations are determined. **And he will enter into a binding and irrevocable covenant with the many for one week (seven years), but in the middle of the week he will stop the sacrifice and grain offering [for the remaining three and one-half years]; and on the wing of abominations will come one who makes desolate, even until the complete destruction, one that is decreed, is poured out on the one who causes the horror.**" (Author's emphasis)

Most Bible scholars break these 'seventy weeks' down into three distinct periods, using the method of the weeks to mean years, as follows:

1) The first set of 7 x 7 weeks being 49 years from the time the decree was given to rebuild Jerusalem until its completion.

2) From that point, the second set of 62 x 7 weeks being the 434 years waiting for the Anointed One to appear. This would be the Messiah, Jesus Christ. After those 434 years, the Anointed One would be cut off (crucified), and then Jerusalem would be destroyed again, which occurred in 70 AD.

3) The final set of 1 x 7 weeks being the final period of 7 years of the Great Tribulation; the time of the Antichrist's arising and his signing of a 7-year covenant with 'many', and the pouring out of the great wrath of God on the world of unbelievers, culminating in Jesus' Second Coming. We will look at all of these later in this book.

Since the time of Jesus' crucifixion in the 69th week of the prophecy given to Daniel, the world has been living in a 'gap' pending the arrival of the final 7 years of the Great Tribulation. This gap is what scholars call the 'Church Age' or the 'Age of Grace'; a period of time where the Church has been commissioned by Christ to preach the Gospel to the nations. At an appointed time, God will bring this time of His grace to an end. At that time, He will remove the Church (followers of Christ) from the earth and begin the outpouring of His wrath upon all who have rejected Christ.

It is clear that the highlighted part at the end of the scripture passage (Daniel 9:20-27) occurs at a future appointed time after Jesus' crucifixion. It is also clear that it relates to the 7-year Tribulation period. The person to whom these emphasised verses refer will make a 7-year covenant with 'many' (presumably many nations). It is without doubt that all of the first 69 weeks have been fulfilled, but this final part of the making of a 7-year covenant 'with many' has not ever been fulfilled in history.

But rather interestingly, after over 70 years of hostility from many nations towards Israel since it became a nation again on 14th May 1948, a peace deal between Israel, the United Arab Emirates and Bahrain has been agreed and was signed on 15th September

2020. Israeli Prime Minister, Benjamin Netanyahu, has stated that he is very optimistic that other Arab nations will join this agreement. Whether this is the fulfilment of the 7-year covenant of Daniel's prophecy is yet to be seen, but one would have to say that this is a monumental shift in world events relating to Israel; the nation that, since 1948, much of the world has been hostile towards and many would prefer to see it wiped off the map. We will be looking at this peace treaty later, in Chapter 4.

Next, I want to show two passages in Daniel chapter 11 which mention the rise of the Antichrist, and what he will do;

"Armed forces of his will arise [in Jerusalem] and defile *and* desecrate the sanctuary, the [spiritual] stronghold, and will do away with the regular sacrifice [that is, the daily burnt offering]; and they will set up [a pagan altar in the sanctuary which is] the abomination of desolation. With smooth *words* [of flattery and praise] he will turn to godlessness those who [are willing to] disregard the [Mosaic] covenant, but the people who [are spiritually mature and] know their God will display strength and take action [to resist]." – Daniel 11:31-32 AMP

"Then the king (the Antichrist) will do exactly as he pleases; he will exalt himself and magnify himself above every god and will speak astounding *and* disgusting things against the God of gods and he will prosper until the indignation is finished, for that which is determined [by God] will be done." – Daniel 11:36 AMP

I would also encourage you to read Daniel chapter 12 for additional study about the time of the end.

Later on in this book we will see that the content of these prophecies in the Book of Daniel are confirmed by the End Times vision given by Jesus to the angel of the Lord to reveal to the Apostle John in the Book of Revelation.

But now we will look at how the Antichrist is mentioned in the New Testament.

Chapter 3

THE ANTICHRIST –
ACCORDING TO THE NEW TESTAMENT

In the following two verses, Jesus indicates that there will be a fulfillment of the Antichrist in a specific person who is to come:

"…for the ruler of this world is coming…" – John 14:30 ESV

"I have come in my Father's name, and you do not receive me; if another comes in his own name, him you will receive." – John 5:43 NKJV

This world has rejected the true Messiah, Jesus Christ, and persecutes His followers with a hatred that knows no bounds. It is manifesting in a raging lawlessness, which we will look at in Chapter 4. Yet with the escalation of End Times signs that are engulfing the planet, in order to get this world out of global chaos, a figure will arise whom the people will hail as their 'saviour'. They don't want Jesus as their Saviour to set them free from their sins and give them eternal life; they want someone who will promise to save them from the chaos and restore this world to a form of 'normality'. The world will *receive* this person and worship him for 'saving the world'.

In the passage below, the Apostle John tells us that this world is fading away, along with everything that people crave, and this certainly is the case with all that is happening in 2020. This leads him to warn of the coming Antichrist.

"Do not love this world nor the things it offers you, for when you love the world, you do not have the love of the Father in you. For the world offers only a craving for physical pleasure, a craving for everything we see, and pride in our achievements and possessions. These are not from the Father, but are from this world. And this world is fading away, along with everything that people crave. But anyone who does what pleases God will live forever.

Dear children, the last hour is here. **You have heard that the Antichrist is coming, and already many such antichrists have appeared.** From this we know that the last hour has come." – 1 John 2:15-18 NLT (Author's emphasis)

In the Amplified Bible translation of the highlighted text above (verse 18), it defines the Antichrist in more detail;

"Children, it is the last hour [the end of this age]; and just as you heard **that the antichrist is coming [the one who will oppose Christ and attempt to replace Him]**, even now many antichrists (false teachers) have appeared, which confirms our belief that it is the last hour." (Author's emphasis)

John reveals more about the Antichrist:

"So I am writing to you not because you don't know the truth but because you know the difference between truth and lies. And who is a liar? **Anyone who says that Jesus is not the Christ. Anyone who denies the Father and the Son is an antichrist.** Anyone who denies the Son doesn't have the Father, either." – 1 John 2:21-23(a) NLT (Author's emphasis)

"This is how we know if they have the Spirit of God: If a person claiming to be a prophet acknowledges that Jesus Christ came in a real body, that person has the Spirit of

God. But if someone claims to be a prophet and does not acknowledge the truth about Jesus, that person is not from God. **Such a person has the spirit of the Antichrist, which you heard is coming into the world and indeed is already here.**" – 1 John 4:2-3 NLT (Author's emphasis)

"I say this because many deceivers, who do not acknowledge Jesus Christ as coming in the flesh, have gone out into the world. **Any such person is the deceiver and the antichrist.**" – 2 John 1:7 NIV (Author's emphasis)

In the next passage, the Apostle Paul warns of the coming of the Antichrist:

"Now in regard to the coming of our Lord Jesus Christ and our gathering together to meet Him, we ask you, brothers and sisters, not to be quickly unsettled or alarmed either by a [so-called prophetic revelation of a] spirit or a message or a letter [alleged to be] from us, to the effect that the day of the Lord has [already] come. Let no one in any way deceive or entrap you, for that day will not come unless the apostasy comes first [that is, the great rebellion, the abandonment of the faith by professed Christians] and the man of lawlessness is revealed, the son of destruction [the Antichrist, the one who is destined to be destroyed], who opposes and exalts himself [so proudly and so insolently] above every so-called god or object of worship, so that he [actually enters and] takes his seat in the temple of God, publicly proclaiming that he himself is God. Do you not remember that when I was still with you, I was telling you these things? And you know what restrains him now [from being revealed]; it is so that he will be revealed at his own [appointed] time. For the mystery of lawlessness [rebellion against divine authority and the coming reign of lawlessness] is already

at work; [but it is restrained] only until he who now restrains it is taken out of the way. Then the lawless one [the Antichrist] will be revealed and the Lord Jesus will slay him with the breath of His mouth and bring him to an end by the appearance of His coming. The coming of the [Antichrist, the lawless] one is through the activity of Satan, [attended] with great power [all kinds of counterfeit miracles] and [deceptive] signs and false wonders [all of them lies], and by unlimited seduction to evil and with all the deception of wickedness for those who are perishing, because they did not welcome the love of the truth [of the gospel] so as to be saved [they were spiritually blind, and rejected the truth that would have saved them]."
– 2 Thessalonians 2:1-10 AMP

From these passages, we can see that before the final End Times Antichrist actually appears, the spirit of the Antichrist will be evident in this world. Quite forcefully, the Apostle John tells us that anyone who denies the Father and His Son Jesus Christ, is an antichrist! When we think how many different religions there are in the 21st century which deny God as the Father and also deny that Jesus Christ is the Messiah, this world is literally full to the brim with people who, John is saying, are an antichrist; they are people who have the spirit of the antichrist, even though they may not realise or accept this to be the case.

It is absolutely clear from scripture that if anyone denies either God the Father or His son Jesus Christ (or both), they are an embodiment of the Antichrist.

Since the creation of the world, the satanic spirit of the Antichrist has been in this world, but the passages above show us that *the Antichrist* himself is coming. We will study this in the next chapter.

Let's look at some other names or descriptions of the Antichrist, remembering that he is the embodiment of Satan.

The god/ruler of this world

"Now judgment is upon this world [the sentence is being passed]. Now the ruler of this world (Satan) will be cast out." – John 12:31 AMP

"...the god of this world [Satan] has blinded the minds of the unbelieving to prevent them from seeing the illuminating light of the gospel of the glory of Christ, who is the image of God." – 2 Corinthians 4:4 AMP

The prince of the power of the air

"...You were following the ways of this world [influenced by this present age], in accordance with the prince of the power of the air (Satan), the spirit who is now at work in the disobedient [the unbelieving, who fight against the purposes of God]." – Ephesians 2:2 AMP

Spiritual forces of wickedness

"For our struggle is not against flesh and blood [contending only with physical opponents], but against the rulers, against the powers, against the world forces of this [present] darkness, against the spiritual forces of wickedness in the heavenly (supernatural) places."
– Ephesians 6:12 AMP

An angel of light

"And no wonder, since Satan himself masquerades as an angel of light.

So it is no great surprise if his servants also masquerade as servants of righteousness, but their end will correspond with their deeds." – 2 Corinthians 11:14-15 AMP

The devil

"Because God's children are human beings—made of flesh and blood—the Son also became flesh and blood. For only as a human being could he die, and only by dying could he break the power of the devil, who had the power of death." – Hebrews 2:14 NLT

"So humble yourselves before God. Resist the devil, and he will flee from you." – James 4:7 NLT

"Stay alert! Watch out for your great enemy, the devil. He prowls around like a roaring lion, looking for someone to devour." – 1 Peter 5:8 NLT

"But when people keep on sinning, it shows that they belong to the devil, who has been sinning since the beginning. But the Son of God came to destroy the works of the devil." – 1 John 3:8 NLT

"So now we can tell who are children of God and who are children of the devil. Anyone who does not live righteously and does not love other believers does not belong to God." – 1 John 3:10 NLT

From these passages, we can see the evidence of Satan's relentless plan to destroy humanity. But if we humble ourselves before God, and resist the devil, he will flee from us. Ultimately, we can see that Jesus came to destroy the works of the devil, and by His dying on the cross, Jesus has indeed broken the power of the devil, whose plan has been to destroy all who turn to Christ for their salvation. Satan's (the Antichrist's) whole blood-thirsty desire is that *no one* should repent and that *all* should perish and join him in the lake of fire. But God's desire is that *none* should perish and that *all* would come to repentance and put their faith in His Son Jesus Christ to save them and enjoy eternal life in the kingdom of heaven (see 2 Peter 3:9 & John 3:16). What a contrast! Yet the choice is left to us as to whom we will follow. Jesus confirmed this very fact:

"You can enter God's Kingdom only through the narrow gate. The highway to hell is broad, and its gate is wide for the many who choose that way. But the gateway to life is very narrow and the road is difficult, and only a few ever find it." – Matthew 7:13-14 NLT

We will look at making this choice in the Epilogue.

But in the next chapter we are going to study the signs of the End Times.

Chapter 4

SIGNS OF THE END TIMES

"...Tell us, when will all this happen? What sign will signal your return and the end of the world?" – Matthew 24:3 NLT

Section A – What's going on?

A quick internet search for 'signs of the End Times' or 'the end of the world' will bring up a whole host of articles and videos that may well overwhelm you, although much of what is offered is often based on a secular and non-biblical viewpoint. It would seem that millions of people are interested in what appears to be one of the hottest topics of the century, all searching for something that will help them make sense of the chaos that the world is now experiencing.

The purpose of this chapter is to focus on what God's Word has to say about the End Times. The prophets of the Old Testament spoke of these times and, in the New Testament, Jesus warned us of its future reality, as well as the apostles in their epistles to believers. We will look at some of these scriptures further on in this chapter.

Clearly, End Times events are going to happen. God has *not* changed His mind on this. The End Times, and the end of the world as we know it, is the culmination and fulfilment of His eternal plan, and it *will* come to pass. Whilst God's Word says that no one will know when the end will be; not the angels, not even Jesus Himself, but only God (see Matthew 24:36; Mark 13:32), Jesus has told us to look for the *signs* of the End Times.

This chapter will clearly show us what Jesus says will be the signs and evidence of His approaching return. In view of this, perhaps it would be wise to open our eyes and ears and look at what is happening around us in the heavens, on the earth, and in the sea, and weigh up our observations to see if the visible evidence is confirmed in the Bible. As God has said He will bring these things to pass, we cannot afford to continue living with our heads buried in the sand, ignoring the glaringly obvious signs all around us, pretending that all is well in our little world. The truth is, all is *far* from well! Our world is groaning and struggling under the strain of the sin and evil that the human race is inflicting upon it (see Isaiah 24:5). The earth is demonstrating its distress with outward visible signs of destruction, devastation, catastrophe, and collapse on an escalating scale approaching cataclysmic proportions.

A 'Wake Up' Call

In 2008, the Lord began to open my eyes to the unfolding signs of the End Times. I have been a born-again, Spirit-filled believer since 1992, yet up until 2008 I failed to believe that any End Times events could actually occur during my lifetime. I merely assumed that they would occur at some future point in time, long after I had drawn my last breath. I have spent much of my Christian life with a total disregard towards the scriptural exhortation to discern events in relation to the End Times. I have to confess that I had been wrapped up in my own life, not wanting to be troubled by biblical events that would surely never affect my existence.

But the Lord had other plans! In 2009, the Lord gave me the words 'Wake Up, Church!' which, in 2011, brought about the writing of my first book, *Come on Church! Wake Up!*

As I mentioned in the Introduction, at the end of each year, I come before the Lord in prayer and ask Him to put into my heart His word for the New Year ahead. For the year 2010, the words 'The Unveiling of Revelation' were what I felt the Holy Spirit say to me. The experience was so profound that it was as if the Lord was saying to me that what was written in the Book of Revelation would begin to be 'unveiled' and poured out upon the earth, starting with the opening of the seals in Revelation chapter 6. I have no idea why the Lord would say such a thing to me, but He did, and the sense of foreboding contained in those words brought a deep reverential fear upon me; an experience which remains in me to this day.

Since that time, I have sought the Lord at each New Year for His description of where things are at from a global perspective. For 2011 the description given was 'Death and Destruction,' and for 2012 the description the Lord gave to me was 'Cataclysmic Collapse'.

Throughout 2011-2012, the words that the TV news anchors frequently used to describe events around the world were 'death and destruction', 'cataclysmic', and 'unprecedented collapse', not just financially but also nationally, socially, morally, and relationally. I regularly undertook internet searches for 'End Times' and a great many of the listings were headed 'Death and Destruction' and 'Global Collapse 2012'. It was as if the earth was finally saying it had had enough and was beginning to unveil the signs of End Times collapse. The word the Lord gave me for 2013 was 'Escalation'. I remember watching the news at that time, and the amount of escalation of collapse and other devastating events that occurred around the world in the first three months of 2013 was truly shocking; almost beyond belief. For 2014 to 2019 the Lord did not give me any further descriptions. Someone once said to me that when the Lord doesn't give you any further information, it means that things will continue on the basis of the *last* word He gave you. So, my assumption has been that those years were a continuance of the escalation in worldwide death, destruction and collapse. Without a doubt we can say this has most definitely been the case.

We are now in 2020, and the signs of the End Times have indeed escalated so much that we surely cannot ignore it. For example, the financial collapse of many European nations over the past 10 years leading them to request repeated bail outs; the immense *Brexit* struggle for the United Kingdom to remove itself from the control of the European Union; the turmoil that the EU is now in following Britain's departure; escalating tension in the Middle East and the evil plans of many nations openly declaring that they want to 'wipe Israel off the map'. These are just a few examples, but we now have something that is affecting almost every nation simultaneously... the Covid19 virus.

End Times Dreams

Over the years, I have often wondered why the Lord gives me vivid words concerning each year ahead. They are a very heavy burden to bear, and I have been left wondering what God wants me to do with the descriptions He gives to me. In addition to this (as well as the Lord giving me the words 'Wake Up, Church!'), between 2008 and 2012, I increasingly had what I can only describe as vivid dreams of the End Times. They increased from one dream per month and ended up occurring one or two times each week. I had never had any dreams like this before 2008. At first, they were so terrifying that I would wake up in a state of fright, thinking that the dream was actually happening in real time. But as they increased in frequency, I realised that the Lord was giving me those dreams for a reason. As best as I can, I will try to explain what I saw in these dreams:

> Many people were going about their daily lives; working, shopping, and families were outside enjoying the sunshine. In each dream I am merely an observer of all that is going on around me. Then all of a sudden, catastrophic events start occurring; everyone is panicking and screaming, desperate to know what is happening. Whilst I am there observing the dramatic change from the normality of

everyday life to this sudden chaos, for some reason people begin to rush at me, even begging me to tell them what is going on! Filled with great boldness (which is not typical of my human nature), I begin shouting to everyone that what is happening is the fulfilment of Bible prophecy concerning the End Times signs of the approaching return of Jesus; signs which will precede the final end of the world as we currently know it.

In every dream, the Lord empowers me to speak with His authority about these things in order to tell the people that, should they not survive these events, if they do not know Jesus Christ as their Lord and Saviour, they will end up in hell. I keep repeating the message to all these people over and over again, emphasizing that God's Word says that they will not enter the kingdom of heaven if they have not been born again (see John 3:1–8).

In these dreams I am informing the people about the Rapture of true believers, and about complacent, half-hearted believers being left behind on the earth to endure the Great Tribulation period which will occur after the Rapture. I then find that I am warning them about the rise of a New World Order which will consist of an alliance of nations led by the Antichrist, a global currency, and a One World Religion. The New World Order will control the whole world (see Revelation 13:11-18; 17:1-18).

All I seem to do in these dreams is warn everyone of what is to come. I am not given to see any fruit borne from speaking this message; I do not see anyone respond to it with confession and repentance. The people just listen to it while they rush around in a terrified panic.

At the time of having all these dreams, to my great shame I had never really had any interest in reading the Book of Revelation. I really did not know much about what God's Word said concerning the End Times; certainly not about a New World Order, One World Religion or a global currency, so I was quite shocked that I was saying all these things in these dreams. This is what God used to begin opening my eyes. I was a complacent Christian living my life more for the things of this world than I was for Christ. It was as if the Lord was showing me what was coming in order to wake *me* up out of my own spiritual slumber. It certainly did the trick because from that moment on, my life changed dramatically.

A New Perspective

From the moment I started having those dreams, I felt that the Lord caused the 'veil to drop' or the 'scales' to fall from my eyes. I now observe life very differently from the way I used to. I look at everything in life from the eternal perspective. Whilst God's Word says He will not reveal when the end of the world will be, He *does* want His children to open their eyes, look around them, and discern if what they are seeing is a fulfilment of His Word in relation to End Times. Jesus has told us that we need to be *so* observant that we will actually know when His return is 'at the door' (see Matthew 24:33; Mark 13:29).

This prolonged period of dreams brought about the writing of my second book, *The End of the World,* which you will find listed at the back of this book. The dreams stopped abruptly the moment that I started writing that book back in 2013. Since that time, I have been simply observing what is happening upon the earth and searching the scriptures about them. I have tried to verbalize to other believers the things that I am seeing, but most of them have stared at me as if I am crazy and they have hastily changed the subject. However, a small number of believers have fully understood.

It has been hard for me to grasp the fact that many brothers and sisters in Christ do not seem interested or concerned in the slightest about the staggering, escalating, global evidence of End Times signs occurring on the earth, in the heavens, and in the sea. I am left with the silent question inside me, asking, "Why do those who profess to be followers of Christ not want to believe that the End Times that Jesus speaks about could actually occur in our current lifetime?" It would seem that many believers live their lives as if it will never occur. At best, it is often treated as if it is a fairy tale; but at times the subject is responded to with disdain. Let me repeat—the End Times events and the culminating end of the world is the fulfilment of the will of God. It is about the Second Coming of His Son, Jesus Christ, the end of this existing world, and the coming of the new heaven, the new earth and the New Jerusalem. This ought to make believers excited and eager to be watchful for the signs of His approaching return and make themselves ready for that glorious day.

At that appointed time, Jesus will come to redeem those who have put their faith and trust in Him as their Lord and Saviour and are living their lives on this earth in obedience to His Word. As believers, we ought to be diligent and vigilant in our watch for the signs of the return of our Bridegroom. We cannot claim to be ready for Jesus' return if we are failing to observe and discern what is happening in the world. While many followers of Christ seem to be half asleep where this vital issue is concerned, it is staggering that many *unbelievers* seem to be very interested in the subject of the end of the world yet they *will not* accept that Jesus Christ has got anything to do with it!

As we will see later in this book, Jesus makes it clear in scripture that those who do not believe in Him or who have rejected Him will not enter the kingdom of heaven. God's holy Word makes it abundantly clear that their eternal end will be in the lake of fire (see Revelation 20:15). These are God's words, not mine.

To simply be interested in the subject of the End Times but not come to the conclusion that we need to confess our sins, repent of them, and turn to Jesus to save us from eternity in hell, is *utter* futility. If one is not a believer, what is the point of being interested in the End Times when the fulfilment of it will catapult one's soul into eternal hell?

Hell

I have heard many Christian leaders say that hell is *merely* eternal separation from God. When I have heard such preaching with no further explanation from the preacher, I have felt the piercing sword of the Holy Spirit prompting me deep within to make a note that while what was preached was technically true, it was not the whole truth. Left as it is, it deceives people into thinking that they will be okay being 'separated from God for eternity'. Bear in mind that a large percentage of the global population are quite content living their earthly lives without God, and would no doubt conclude that it is no big deal for them to live without God for eternity either.

For the Church to reduce the horrific reality of spending eternity in hell down to a weak and powerless statement that hell is *merely* eternal separation from God, is to abandon the duty that God has placed upon the Church. That duty is to bear witness not only to the Cross of Christ and the Gospel message of salvation through faith in Jesus Christ, but also to the full reality of eternal torment of hell for all who refuse to believe that Jesus came to save them from spending eternity in that horrific place.

The New Testament is packed with scriptures of what hell is like. Most of these are spoken by Jesus Himself. How have we ended up in the situation where leaders in the Church think nothing about reducing eternity in hell to such a trivial and powerless statement?! How will unbelievers ever escape from the outcome of eternal torment in hell if the Church fails to preach to them the realities of such an end, as clearly written down in the Word of God? These powerful scriptures are written in the Bible for us to preach so that unbelievers will wake up when they hear what awaits them if they remain an unbeliever.

The realities of hell *also* need to be preached to believers to encourage them to remain obedient to God's Word, because the consequences of backsliding and remaining in a state of rebellion and unrepentance, are the same as the consequences for unbelievers.

How the Lord must grieve when He hears His Church water down the truth about hell, when His love for all mankind compelled Him to send His Son, Jesus Christ, to die on the cross and shed His blood so that the way would be opened for the whole human race (if they will believe in Jesus) to be saved from experiencing such devastating eternal consequences.

I also hear preachers say, "We don't want to frighten people into believing." This is quite shocking. I don't think the early Christians had this mindset. Our church leaders need to grasp the fact that spending eternity in hell is something *everyone* ought to be frightened of, so it ought to be preached! The truth about hell is written in the Holy Bible, and so we are without excuse. When we believe that hell does not exist, we are declaring Jesus to be a liar. Have we no conscience that would cause us to tremble in fear of His holy and righteous judgement? Have we no shame that our preaching of such false doctrine will lead multitudes of people to ultimately end in eternal torment in hell?

The Lord says, through the prophet Jeremiah,

> 'How can you say, "We are wise because we have the word of the Lord," when your teachers have twisted it by writing lies? These wise teachers will fall into the trap of their own foolishness, for they have rejected the word of the Lord. Are they so wise after all?'—Jeremiah 8:8–9 NLT

But even though, throughout the centuries, many true and faithful servants of the Lord have proclaimed God's warnings to the world, still the world will not listen; still it will not respond. Regardless of this fact, these warnings must still be preached.

"So you shall speak all these words to them, but they will

not listen to you. You shall call to them, but they will not answer you. And you shall say to them, 'This is the nation that did not obey the voice of the LORD their God, and did not accept discipline; truth has perished; it is cut off from their lips.' " – Jeremiah 7:27-28 ESV

"But if any nation will not listen, then I will utterly pluck it up and destroy it, declares the LORD." – Jeremiah 12:17 ESV

"And if any place will not receive you and they will not listen to you, when you leave, shake off the dust that is on your feet as a testimony against them." – Mark 6:11 ESV

Won't we all go to heaven?

With many church leaders being afraid to preach about hell, this has given rise to false doctrine being preached which deceives people into believing that everyone will enter the kingdom of heaven regardless of whom or what they believe, or don't believe. This 'doctrine' makes a mockery of Christ's crucifixion on the cross. It is the teaching of wolves in sheep's clothing; church leaders who are workers for the prince of darkness, who we have seen is the devil, Satan, the Antichrist.

Concerning the reality of hell, in his book *Are You Ready for the End of Time? Understanding Future Events from Prophetic Passages of the Bible,* J.C. Ryle, the first Bishop of Liverpool from 1880-1900 wrote,

"There is much about *hell* in Revelation. There are many fearful expressions which show its reality, its misery, its eternity, its certainty. How deeply important it is to have clear views on this solemn subject in the present day! A disposition appears in some quarters to shrink from asserting the eternity of punishment. A flood of that miserable heresy, universalism, seems coming in upon us… Tender-hearted women and intellectual men are catching at the theory that, after all, there is hope in the far distance for everybody, and that Satan's old assertion deserves credit, 'Ye shall not surely die.' Oh, reader, beware of this delusion!" [1]

Even though Ryle wrote these words in the 19th century, how well they apply to our current times, and how right that he uses the word *theory* in relation to the doctrine of Universalism. Many people believe that when their mortal flesh dies, that's the end of life. They don't believe that they have a soul that will rise from their body and will live for eternity in heaven or in hell. There are some who believe that when they die, their soul will come back to life in some other form, and when that form then dies, their soul will move on again into another life form in a never ending cycle of life, supposedly for the soul to learn something that they may have failed to fully learn in their 'previous lives.'

All of this is contrary to the Word of God. Physical death will come to us all, and the Word of God says that we are appointed to die once, and after that comes the judgement (see Hebrews 9:27). His Word also says we will all stand before the judgement seat of Christ and will have to give account of what we have done with our life on earth (see Romans 14:10-12).

> "None of us can hold back our spirit from departing. None of us has the power to prevent the day of our death. There is no escaping that obligation, that dark battle. And in the face of death, wickedness will not come to the rescue of the wicked." – Ecclesiastes 8:8 NLT

None of us will escape that 'divine appointment', that day of reckoning. It would do us well to examine the scriptures concerning the End Times events, in which the Antichrist will play his part. All of it is leading up to this fearful Day of Judgement.

The End Times

I have heard many people say things like, "Every generation thinks it is living in the End Times. So why should we believe that this current 21st century generation has any claim on it?"

It is a biblical fact that this world has been living in the End Times from the moment that Jesus ascended into heaven. So yes, it is true that every generation has been living in the End Times! It is the period of time from His ascension and leading up to His Second Coming. Everything that occurs in this period of time can be classed as fulfilling End Times prophecy. But there has to come a point where the signs of the End Times escalate and converge to such a degree that we cannot shrug it all off as simply the effects of 'global warming' or 'climate change' - although these terms are being used by world governments to bring about their agenda of global control.

God warned us in the Old Testament that a time will come when He will shake the nations. It would seem that, in 2020, we are in a time of unrelenting shaking.

The Great Shaking

"They shall go into the holes of the rocks,
And into the caves of the earth,
From the terror of the LORD
And the glory of His majesty,
When He arises to shake the earth mightily." – Isaiah 2:19
NKJV

"Therefore I will make the heavens tremble,
and the earth will be shaken out of its place,
at the wrath of the LORD of hosts
in the day of his fierce anger." – Isaiah 13:13 ESV

"Behold, the LORD will empty the earth and make it desolate,
and he will twist its surface and scatter its inhabitants.
And it shall be, as with the people, so with the priest;
as with the slave, so with his master;
as with the maid, so with her mistress;
as with the buyer, so with the seller;
as with the lender, so with the borrower;
as with the creditor, so with the debtor.
The earth shall be utterly empty and utterly plundered;
for the LORD has spoken this word.
"The earth mourns and withers;
the world languishes and withers;
the highest people of the earth languish.
The earth lies defiled
under its inhabitants;
for they have transgressed the laws,
violated the statutes,
broken the everlasting covenant.
Therefore a curse devours the earth,
and its inhabitants suffer for their guilt;
therefore the inhabitants of the earth are scorched,
and few men are left.
The wine mourns,
the vine languishes,
all the merry-hearted sigh.
The mirth of the tambourines is stilled,
the noise of the jubilant has ceased,
the mirth of the lyre is stilled.
No more do they drink wine with singing;
strong drink is bitter to those who drink it.
The wasted city is broken down;
every house is shut up so that none can enter."
– Isaiah 24:1-10 ESV

"Terror and the pit and the snare
are upon you, O inhabitant of the earth!
He who flees at the sound of the terror
shall fall into the pit,
and he who climbs out of the pit
shall be caught in the snare.
For the windows of heaven are opened,
and the foundations of the earth tremble.
The earth is utterly broken,
the earth is split apart,
the earth is violently shaken." – Isaiah 24:17-19 ESV

"For thus says the LORD of hosts: Yet once more, in a little while, I will shake the heavens and the earth and the sea and the dry land." – Haggai 2:6 ESV

Jesus warned us about this shaking too;

"And there will be signs in the sun, in the moon, and in the stars; and on the earth distress of nations, with perplexity, the sea and the waves roaring; men's hearts failing them from fear and the expectation of those things which are coming on the earth, for the powers of the heavens will be shaken. Then they will see the Son of Man coming in a cloud with power and great glory." – Luke 21:25-27 NKJV

And also, the writer to the Hebrews says;

"See that you do not refuse him who is speaking. For if they did not escape when they refused him who warned them on earth, much less will we escape if we reject him who warns from heaven. At that time his voice shook the earth, but now he has promised, "Yet once more I will shake not only the earth but also the heavens." This phrase, "Yet once more," indicates the removal of things

that are shaken—that is, things that have been made—in order that the things that cannot be shaken may remain."
– Hebrews 12:25-27 ESV

The earth itself is groaning under the weight of humanity's sin, waiting for its redemption;

"The earth suffers for the sins of its people, for they have twisted God's instructions, violated his laws, and broken his everlasting covenant." – Isaiah 24:5 NLT

"...Because there is no faithfulness [no steadfast love, no dependability] or loyalty or kindness. Or knowledge of God [from personal experience with Him] in the land. There is [false] swearing of oaths, deception (broken faith), murder, stealing, and adultery; They employ violence, so that one [act of] bloodshed follows closely on another. Therefore the land [continually] mourns, And everyone who lives in it languishes [in tragic suffering] Together with the animals of the open country and the birds of the heavens; Even the fish of the sea disappear."
– Hosea 4:1(b) - 3 AMP

"For [even the whole] creation [all nature] waits eagerly for the children of God to be revealed. For the creation was subjected to frustration and futility, not willingly [because of some intentional fault on its part], but by the will of Him who subjected it, in hope that the creation itself will also be freed from its bondage to decay [and gain entrance] into the glorious freedom of the children of God. For we know that the whole creation has been moaning together as in the pains of childbirth until now. And not only this, but we too, who have the first fruits of the Spirit [a joyful indication of the blessings to come], even we groan inwardly, as we wait eagerly for [the sign of] our adoption as sons—the redemption and transformation of our body [at the resurrection]."
– Romans 8:19-23 AMP

The big rush, and the increase in knowledge

In the Book of Daniel, we see the angel of the Lord telling him of a particular sign that will indicate when this world is at the time of the end:

> "But you, Daniel, keep this prophecy a secret; **seal up the book until the time of the end, when many will rush here and there, and knowledge will increase.**" – Daniel 12:4 NLT (Author's emphasis)

This passage is very interesting as Daniel is told that the 'time of the end' would be marked by a sign of people *rushing here and there, and when knowledge would increase.*

'Rushing here and there' would seem to describe an increase in the desire or need for travel. This was made possible in the early 20th century with the manufacture of motor cars, and later, aircraft, which led to the rise in global travel becoming easy by the 1970s. Each decade has seen an increase in travel, with the need for some international airports to extend their runway capacity to cope with the increasing demand.

With the invention of the computer, and later, the arrival of the internet in the early 2000's, the ability to obtain knowledge has sky-rocketed. Whatever we wish to know is now available at the touch of a button on a variety of devices, and now including smart watches. What was once only available on a rather large dial-up computer is now accessible on a small wristwatch. Soon all this information will be accessible on a tiny microchip implanted under our skin.

Feeling worn out?

The angel of the Lord also told Daniel that during the End Times, the relentless activity of the forces of darkness will over-power and wear out the saints. Whilst the passage below relates to the Antichrist wearing down those who become followers of Christ during the Great Tribulation, I think we would agree that in the build up to the arrival of the man who will be the Antichrist, the spirit of the Antichrist that is now invading the earth is causing immense weariness to come upon many believers around the world. My husband and I are certainly feeling this, as are many of our Christian friends. Add to this the sudden global shaking that is now happening, it seems that this weariness has increased exponentially in 2020.

> "As I kept looking, that horn **was making war with the saints (believers) and overpowering them** until the Ancient of Days came and judgment was passed in favor of the saints of the Most High [God], and the time arrived when the saints (believers) took possession of the kingdom." – Daniel 7:21-22 AMP (Author's emphasis)

> "He will speak words against the Most High [God] **and wear down the saints of the Most High…**" – Daniel 7:25(a) AMP (Author's emphasis)

All creatures, great and small

We also see indications of the extreme suffering of the creatures of this earth, and mass animal die-off:

> "How the animals groan!
> The herds of cattle are bewildered and wander aimlessly
> Because they have no pasture;
> Even the flocks of sheep suffer.

> O LORD, I cry out to You,
> For fire has devoured the pastures of the wilderness,
> And the flame has burned up all the trees of the field.

> Even the wild animals pant [in longing] for You;
> For the water brooks are dried up
> And fire has consumed the pastures of the wilderness."
> – Joel 1:18-20 AMP

> "Therefore the land [continually] mourns,

And everyone who lives in it languishes [in tragic suffering]
Together with the animals of the open country and the birds of the heavens;
Even the fish of the sea disappear." – Hosea 4:3 AMP

"I will completely consume *and* sweep away all things
From the face of the earth [in judgment]," says the LORD.
"I will consume *and* sweep away man and beast;
I will consume *and* sweep away the birds of the air
And the fish of the sea..." – Zephaniah 1:2-3(a) AMP

And as we would expect, this is heightened in the Book of Revelation:

"The second angel sounded [his trumpet], and something like a great mountain blazing with fire was hurled into the sea; and a third of the sea was turned to blood; and a third of the living creatures that were in the sea died, and a third of the ships were destroyed." – Revelation 8:8-9 AMP.

I came across a website, www.bibleprophecytruth.com which keeps a track on occurrences of mass die-off. It is quite shocking to see the increase in incidents of God's creatures, great and small, dying in huge numbers without any explanation; thousands of fish, whales, dolphins, seals, birds, cattle, sheep and pigs, as well as a variety of insects. There are many videos on YouTube, if you are interested in researching this for yourself.

Section B – What Jesus says about the End Times

Moving now to the New Testament let's see what is written about the End Times. Before Jesus was crucified, He shared with His disciples the details of events that would occur which would indicate the sign that His return was near, even 'at the door' (see Mark 13:29).

We will start by looking at what Jesus says concerning the first stages of these events, referred to in some translations as the 'birth pains', or 'the beginning of sorrows', but in the Amplified Bible translation below, Jesus refers to these times as the 'birth pangs';

'Jesus left the temple *area* and was going on His way when His disciples came up to Him to call His attention to the [magnificent and massive] buildings of the temple. And He said to them, "Do you see all these things? I assure you *and* most solemnly say to you, not one stone here will be left on another, which will not be torn down."

While Jesus was seated on the Mount of Olives, the disciples came to Him privately, and said, "Tell us, when will this [destruction of the temple] take place, and what will be the sign of Your coming, and of the end (completion, consummation) of the age?"

Jesus answered, "Be careful that no one misleads you [deceiving you and leading you into error]. For many will come in My name [misusing it, and appropriating the strength of the name which belongs to Me], saying, 'I am the Christ (the Messiah, the Anointed),' and they will mislead many. You will *continually* hear of wars and rumors of wars. See that you are not frightened, for *those things* must take place, but that is not yet the end [of the age]. For nation will rise against nation, and kingdom against kingdom, and there will be famines and earthquakes in various places. But all these things are merely the beginning of birth pangs [of the intolerable anguish and the time of unprecedented trouble].

"Then they will hand you over to [endure] tribulation, and will put you to death, and you will be hated by all nations because of My name. At that time many will be offended *and* repelled [by their association with Me] and will fall away [from the One whom they should trust] and will betray one another [handing over believers to their persecutors] *and* will hate one another. Many false prophets will appear and mislead many. Because lawlessness is increased, the love of most people will grow cold. But the one who endures *and* bears up [under suffering] to the end will be saved. This good news of the kingdom [the gospel] will be preached throughout the whole world as a testimony to all the nations, and then the end [of the age] will come." ' – Matthew 24:1-14 AMP

Let's break this passage down to see if any of the things Jesus is saying about the End Times signs are actually occurring today.

The Destruction of the Temple

Jesus firstly warned the people that the temple of God would be destroyed. This happened in 70 AD and the people of Israel were scattered into exile across the world, and the land of Israel remained a desolate wasteland until, by the miraculous hand of God, it was restored to them in a single day, on 14th May 1948, and her 'children' have been gradually returning to their nation since that monumental day. Their return to their homeland has escalated in very recent years. This event fulfils the Old Testament prophecy spoken by the prophet Isaiah:

"Before the birth pains even begin,
Jerusalem gives birth to a son.
Who has ever seen anything as strange as this?
Who ever heard of such a thing?
Has a nation ever been born in a single day?
Has a country ever come forth in a mere moment?
But by the time Jerusalem's birth pains begin,
her children will be born.
Would I ever bring this nation to the point of birth
and then not deliver it?" asks the LORD.
"No! I would never keep this nation from being born,"
says your God." – Isaiah 66:7-9 NLT

But the temple has never been rebuilt.

False messiahs

Then Jesus tells his disciples of the things that will happen on the earth signifying that His return is near. He mentions the rise of false messiahs; people claiming to be the Second Coming of Jesus. This has been happening throughout the centuries but has escalated in recent years. An online search will give you examples of this, so I won't list any here, although I have done so in my book *Watchmen...or Wolves?* (which I co-authored with my husband, Chris) the details of which are contained at the back of this book.

Natural Disasters

Jesus then tells them of natural disasters that will come. He refers to these as the beginning of 'birth pains' which will *precede* the time of intolerable anguish and unprecedented trouble; which the Church calls the time of the Great Tribulation. This world has been experiencing these 'birth pain' events in gradual doses, spaced out over the many centuries since Christ spoke these words. But I am sure that we would all agree that since the return of the people to the nation of Israel in 1948, these birth pain events have increased exponentially in the last few years. It would seem that there is no let-up in their intensity.

In Luke's Gospel, Jesus' account of the End Times events has some additions:

> "Then Jesus told them, "Nation will rise against nation and kingdom against kingdom. There will be violent earthquakes, and in various places famines and [deadly and devastating] **pestilences (plagues, epidemics); and there will be terrible sights and great signs from heaven.**" – Luke 21:10-11 AMP (Author's emphasis)

We would have to be living in the depths of a very dark cave to not notice that these birth pains signs have got to a point where they are converging into an endless torrent of distress in the nations.

Wars, rumours of wars, floods, earthquakes, famines, storms, volcanoes, tornadoes, rivers turning the colour of blood, animals, fish and birds suddenly dying in massive numbers, wildfires raging for months and destroying areas of forest the size of France (which was reported in one article I read), mud slides, sink holes, pestilences (plagues and epidemics) and locust swarms. All of these ever-increasing events can be freely researched on the internet. A valuable source of information on this is the YouTube channel of The Two Preachers. But in view of the Covid19 pestilence which has reduced this world to a state of global lockdown, let's take a quick look at the subject of pestilences.

Pestilences

What is a pestilence? Various online sites define it as any virulent, overwhelming, deadly disease that spreads quickly and kills large numbers of people.

There have been major isolated outbreaks through the centuries, but we have now entered an era where devastating pestilences are occurring annually. Over recent years, we have seen an increase in infectious viruses occurring around the world, such as Ebola, SARS, MERS, Swine flu, Bird flu H1N1, Zika virus, affecting the populations of many nations, although they have stopped short of a global pandemic. But as I mentioned in the Introduction, the world is now in the grip of Covid19, bringing the nations to their knees in their effort to slow its spread. Leaders are commanding their people to stay at home, work from home (if possible), and only go out to the shops to buy essentials. Vast numbers of employees have been put on a temporary leave of absence by their employers, and many have lost their jobs altogether. Some businesses have shut completely and gone bankrupt, and self-employed people are barely able to scrape by on the meagre offerings being handed out by their governments.

Many believe that the Covid19 virus is just a variant of the common winter flu, but in reality, it is far more serious. Some people have been left with long-lasting symptoms such as fatigue, a racing heart, damage to the heart, lungs, kidneys, and brain, shortness of breath, aching joints, brain-fog, and a persistent loss of sense of smell.

Even though it is a real disease with very serious symptoms, its source is still not certain. However, there are suggestions that it is a patented, manufactured virus, which was being tested in China, potentially to be used in biological warfare. Many people dispute this for political reasons, but we cannot dismiss the possibility. Some people believe this to be a conspiracy theory, whilst others offer evidence to support the suggestion.

We will look at this further on in this chapter, in Section D, under the sub-heading **'How did Covid19 appear?'**

Persecution

Returning to the passage in Matthew 24:1-14, after Jesus warns his disciples about the occurrences of natural disasters, He then tells them that they will experience tribulation and be put to death and will be hated by all nations because they are His followers. There is very little reporting on the persecution of Christians on the mainstream media, but social media is a very different matter. There are daily reports of a huge increase in Christians being persecuted for their faith, all around the world. Believers face being sacked from their jobs or taken to Court, and even imprisoned for preaching on the streets. At the extreme, many have lost their lives at the hands of terrorists who hate anyone who proclaims the name of Jesus. In China particularly, persecution of Christians appears limitless. Recent events show that the regime is forcibly removing children from their Christian parents and putting them into government re-education camps to extinguish any Christian teaching they have learnt, and to indoctrinate them with the Chinese totalitarian ideology.

Let's remind ourselves that Jesus Himself said,

"If the world hates you, keep in mind that it hated me first. If you belonged to the world, it would love you as its own. As it is, you do not belong to the world, but I have chosen you out of the world. That is why the world hates you. Remember what I told you: 'A servant is not greater than his master.' If they persecuted me, they will persecute you also. If they obeyed my teaching, they will obey yours also. They will treat you this way because of my name, for they do not know the one who sent me. If I had not come and spoken to them, they would not be guilty of sin; but now they have no excuse for their sin. Whoever hates me hates my Father as well. If I had not done among them the works no one else did, they would not be guilty of sin. As it is, they have seen, and yet they have hated both me and my Father. But this is to fulfill what is written in their Law: 'They hated me without reason.'" – John 15:18-25 NIV

Falling Away

Jesus then warns us that many of His followers will fall away from their faith in Him. It seems staggering that this could happen, but we are certainly living in these times right now. This could be due to the increase in the level of persecution that is happening to Christians. Many believers may feel that they cannot cope with what is happening, and rather than remain firm in their faith and endure the trials during the times of the birth pains, they will abandon their faith in Christ in order to obtain immediate relief from the suffering, ignoring the fact that to abandon their faith will put them in danger of forfeiting their salvation and spending eternity in hell.

In addition to this is the corporate falling away from (or abandonment) of the doctrines of the faith by church leaders which results in the congregation being led astray by the preaching of false gospels. Whether this falling away is individual or corporate, it is known as *apostasy*.

What is Apostasy? Wikipedia describes it as follows;

"Apostasy in Christianity is the rejection of Christianity by someone who formerly was a Christian. The term apostasy comes from the Greek word *apostasia* ("ἀποστασία") meaning defection, departure, revolt or rebellion. It has been described as "a willful falling away from, or rebellion against, Christianity."

(Link: https://en.wikipedia.org/wiki/Apostasy_in_Christianity)

Note the word 'departure' is used in part of the definition. Many in the Church have interpreted this to mean the departure of the Church in the Rapture, but the true implication of the word 'departure' for the word apostasia is in the sense of *departing from our beliefs.*

Whilst speaking of the day of our gathering up to be with the Lord, in the passage below, the Apostle Paul makes it clear that this apostasy (the great falling away from the faith) will occur *first*. Therefore, the word apostasy cannot mean the departure (Rapture) of the Church into heaven. Every sense of the word means an abandonment of faith in Jesus Christ.

"Now in regard to the coming of our Lord Jesus Christ and our gathering together to meet Him, we ask you, brothers and sisters, not to be quickly unsettled or alarmed either by a [so-called prophetic revelation of a] spirit or a message or a letter [alleged to be] from us, to the effect that the day of the Lord has [already] come. Let no one in any way deceive or entrap you, for that day will not come **unless the apostasy comes first [that is, the great rebellion, the abandonment of the faith by professed Christians]…**"
– 2 Thessalonians 2:1-3(a) AMP (Author's emphasis)

In the past decade, the institutional church in the United Kingdom (with a small number of exceptions) has been conspicuous in its failure to speak out against evil and sin, preferring to accept, condone, permit, embrace and celebrate the practices of sin *within* the Church rather than calling sinners to confession, repentance and obedience to God's Word. The Church is demonstrating, both in words and actions, this great falling away from the faith, preferring to engage in the godless practices of the culture of this world, rewriting Church doctrine and sound biblical teaching to accommodate whatever the culture demands. Rather than obeying God's Word and His will, it wants God to bless the will of those who don't want to give up their sinful lives.

The hierarchy in the Church has been derelict in its God-ordained duty to lead the nation and its leaders in the ways of God, thereby causing society to be cast adrift from the moorings of the nation's Christian heritage, leaving its people to flounder in a treacherous ocean of ungodly liberalism. Rather than being God's watchmen over His flock, their apostasy has caused them to become wolves in sheep's clothing.

My husband and I have covered this subject extensively in our co-authored book, *Watchmen... or Wolves?*

For further information on this subject, we would highly recommend reading an eye-opening book by Dr Clifford Hill, *The Reshaping of Britain: Church and State since the 1960s: A Personal Reflection* published by Wilberforce Publications.

Brother betraying Brother

When Jesus refers to 'brother betraying brother', He is referring to believers betraying believers. Around 2,000 years ago, Jesus said that a time will come when those who once proclaimed to be believers will betray and hate those who still are believers, and hand them over to their persecutors. When we observe what is happening today, we can see this alarming situation being fulfilled minute by minute as reports get uploaded onto social media. The level of hostility and hatred that is being hurled by some unrepentant, progressive, liberal Christians (who reject the authority of God's

Word) towards followers of Christ who uphold and obey God's Word, seems to know no bounds.

False prophets

Jesus goes on to inform His disciples that many false prophets will appear and mislead many. False prophets are people who claim they are followers of Christ and speak on behalf of God, but they twist His Word to suit their own understanding, and then preach their false teaching to the congregation. They sound slick and smooth in the presentation and delivery of their poison-laced 'gospels'; indeed, they are so convincing that multitudes are being swallowed up in their deception.

Over the centuries, false prophets have arisen within the Church, but we have reached a time where the Church is inundated with these imposters and is drowning in the deceptions that they peddle. The only way to spot a false prophet - a wolf in sheep's clothing - is to know the Word of God for yourself. It is your weapon against the fiery darts of deceivers, and it is your shield to protect you when you find yourself in their presence. When you know the Word of God, each time a false prophet preaches something that is a twisted version of scripture, you will immediately discern it in your soul. I have experienced this many times over the past 28 years, and I know that it has been the Holy Spirit prodding me and saying, "This is not the truth. Go back to My Word and check it for yourself." I have then done what He has prompted me to do, and sure enough, His Word has proven the 'prophet' to be a liar.

Before we move on to the next part of Jesus' End Times warnings which we are looking at from the passage in Matthew 24, Jesus gives us an additional warning (in Luke 17:1) that a time will come when people will become offended. So, let's look at this briefly.

Taking Offence

'Then said He unto His disciples, "It is impossible but that offences will come, but woe unto him through whom they come!'" – Luke 17:1 KJ21

Prior to the turn of the 21st century, generally speaking, most people would be courteous, considerate and helpful towards others, but would either ignore comments from those who had differing views and opinions to them, or graciously disagree with them. That is the purpose of freedom of speech.

But since the chime of Big Ben hailing in the new millennium on 1st January 2000, something has changed. Humanity has been increasingly showing itself to be full of hatred and hostility, taking offence at almost anything and everything. Over the past few years this has escalated beyond imagination. Not a day goes by without reports of new offences being taken by individuals and groups. Any perceived offence is whipped up into a frenzy, causing many to become caught up in the storm of resentment and anger, often resulting in protests and riots, not just in local areas, but globally. Any tiny little comment by anyone who expresses a view that is contrary to the opinion of the person who feels offended, can result in the person with the differing view being stalked, harassed, verbally and physically abused, and their reputations and careers brought to ruin by the offended person.

Those with differing opinions, views and beliefs to the cultural narrative of our time are now labelled as bigots, racists, misogynists, 'white supremacists' etc. Any view that is expressed which is opposite to the politically correct, ultra-liberal mindset of the millennial age is now being recorded by the police (in the UK) as 'hate-speech'. People have had intimidating, uniformed police officers turn up on their doorsteps or at their places of work, interrogating them about something they have posted on social media at which someone has 'taken offence'. The 'offended' person has then reported it as hate-speech and wants the police to record it as a crime, when in actuality it is merely a difference of opinion, a difference of views or beliefs. In a country where freedom of speech is *still* the law of the land, we should all be perfectly entitled to hold and express differing views without fear of interrogation and arrest.

Many who don't agree with the mindset of those who demand apology and reparation for their perceived grievance, are losing their jobs simply because they expressed a view that is contrary to the 'victim mentality' of our times. This exponential rise in 'taking offence' has reached staggering proportions, leaving thousands of innocent casualties in its wake. This has led to what Jesus warned would also happen in the End Times; a rise in lawlessness.

Lawlessness

This passage of scripture describes all that I have written below:

> "The coming of the lawless one is by the activity of Satan with all power and false signs and wonders, and with all wicked deception for those who are perishing, because they refused to love the truth and so be saved."
> – 2 Thessalonians 2:9-10 ESV

In Western nations, it would be fair to say that, in general, people have been able to go about their daily business without fear and even be able to express their own personal views without anxiety of being attacked or murdered for their beliefs. But since the turn of the 21st century, we have seen an increase in lawlessness with each passing year.

As I type this section in July 2020, the scale of insanity, evil and utter delusion that has invaded humanity is absolutely shocking and terrifying, and is now affecting nations all around the world, not just the West. Jesus said the increase in lawlessness will cause the love of many to grow cold. By this word 'cold' we can assume that people will lose compassion for others; become unfeeling, unmoved by situations, and heartless. Coupled with the rise in taking offence, many with cold hearts could become inflamed with desires to take revenge on what they perceive as an injustice.

There has been a gradual increase in lawlessness since the 1960's, but what we have witnessed in the past few years, and particularly in 2020, is mind-blowing! The world now seems to be a vast cauldron of rebellion; a steaming pressure cooker of hatred and defiance of anything that is sacred, moral, and historically lawful.

A generation of people now exists who think nothing of defying authority and are unwilling to accept that laws exist for the good of all. They are not content to accept that long-held laws are there to protect society and to protect them. They feel aggrieved that such laws prevent them from doing the *unlawful* things they crave, and so they forcefully demand that governing bodies overturn every law that hinders their 'human right' to please themselves in their unlawful behaviour.

Rather than assert their lawfully appointed authority to deal with the unlawful actions of these activists, world governments are caving in under the pressure to appease groups that use violence to force their agenda on the rest of civilisation, pushing for legalisation of just about anything that they demand. Much of what is being pushed and promoted by these large groups is sinful and evil, and the consequence of this is the tidal wave of lawlessness that is now inescapable. Once unlawful things are made lawful, it is almost impossible to make them unlawful again without it causing massive protests and civil commotion from those who insist on being allowed to commit lawlessness. What we are witnessing is summed up in this passage of scripture;

> "The wicked plot against the godly;
> they snarl at them in defiance.
> But the Lord just laughs,
> for he sees their day of judgment coming.
> The wicked draw their swords
> and string their bows
> to kill the poor and the oppressed,
> to slaughter those who do right.

But their swords will stab their own hearts,
and their bows will be broken."
– Psalm 37:12-15 NLT

The following are some of the things we are seeing today which constitute this rise in lawlessness. It is not my intention to go into detail on them, as there is plenty of information on each subject which is freely available on the internet. However, I will make some comments.

1. **Good is now evil, and evil is now good:** It would appear that this world has now reached the stage where much of what was once defined as good, is being overturned by certain groups who wish to redefine what is good and now call it evil, and vice versa (see Isaiah 5:20). We can see this being played out through the LGBTQ+ agenda being heavily promoted in schools (even 'Church' schools), where parents are not being permitted to have their say concerning what their children are being taught in RSE lessons (relationships and sex education). The BBC has recently stated that it wants to play a bigger role in children's education.

   (Link: https://www.telegraph.co.uk/news/2020/07/31/bbc-wants-play-bigger-role-childrens-education/).

   This is an organization which produces resources for schools stating that there are 'over 100 different genders'. They promote twisted programmes as if the contents of these programmes are the truth, pandering to the 21st century narrative of gender fluidity; the idea that we can all be whatever gender we choose to be. What they are actually doing is ditching scientific fact in favour of biased and unsubstantiated opinion.

2. **Paedophilia:** Who would have ever thought that we would reach the time when the evil of paedophilia would even be up for a rethink?! People who have a desire to molest and abuse children in a sexual manner are beginning to make 'human rights' claims that their sexual proclivity be accepted

and normalized. Those who feel a sexual attraction towards children now object to being known as paedophiles because of its historical implication of committing a criminal act. Instead they now wish to be referred to as 'minor attracted persons' (MAP), as if by doing this it somehow lessens the severity of their actions.

3. **Pride parades:** Until the arrival of Covid19, gay Pride parades became prolific in 2019. A march that was previously held on just one day each year rapidly escalated to once a month, then for a weekend, then a whole month, culminating in basically the whole summer being taken over for this event in major cities and towns around the world. With the support, endorsement and even participation of many businesses, organizations, schools, and even the police (who are supposed to be impartial, and are present at these events to ensure law and order is kept), parents are duped into believing it is just a 'nice day out' for the family where their children can wave their rainbow flags. In reality, many videos appearing on social media have revealed parents encouraging their children to participate by touching almost naked men dressed up in perverse costumes that leave nothing to the imagination. The same type of thing is occurring in libraries and other venues with the latest LGBTQ+ activity known as the 'Drag Queen Story Hour', where very young children sit and listen to a gay themed story. Sometimes the person dressed up as the drag queen will laughingly entice the children to touch intimate parts of his anatomy which he may have disguised as a unicorn's horn or a furry snake. The arrival of the Covid19 lockdown has thankfully put a stop to this ungodly indoctrination of our children…but for how long?

These sobering words of Jesus come to mind;

"…but whoever causes one of these little ones who

believe in me to sin, it would be better for him to have a great millstone fastened around his neck and to be drowned in the depth of the sea." – Matthew 18:6 ESV

4. **God removed from society:** Over the past 25 years there has been a gradual removal of Christian assemblies and Christian teaching in schools. In recent years this has escalated to the point where anyone (including students) who hold Christian beliefs are mocked and persecuted, not just by their peers, but also by school staff. Yet at the same time as Christianity is being removed, schools are allowing and promoting anti-Christian material as well as permitting satanic groups to run after-school clubs on the school premises.

In Council chambers, long-established Christian prayers are being stamped out. Instead, invocations to New Age, pagan and satanic 'gods' are being permitted by those presiding over the meetings. And we wonder why society is crumbling in front of our eyes! When a government brings in policies and laws that defy God's Word and permits all manner of evil to usurp the place of God in the land, would He not remove His protection and His blessings from the land if those in authority fail to wake up and repent of their sin? As Psalm 33:12(a) NKJV says, *"Blessed is the nation whose God is the LORD..."*, then we must conclude that He withdraws His blessings from nations that abandon Him and pursue their own godless will. We are witnessing this right across the globe.

5. **The entertainment industry:** This has always been known for pushing the boundaries, but now both Hollywood and the general television industry are bringing sexual orientation and gender identity into almost every area of production. Television advertising is overloaded with images relating

to sexual identity and orientation, and even programmes about house-hunting or the countryside are now injected with some aspect of the LGBTQ + agenda, causing viewers to inundate the TV stations' email inboxes with complaints. This same agenda is now being seen in the main characters of films, particularly those aimed at young children. Not only that, Hollywood is producing a new movie titled *Habit*, with Jesus portrayed as a lesbian, and being played by a female actress. I dare not imagine what the physical and eternal consequences will be for those involved in this blasphemy.

6. **Killing Jesus:** Celebrities and atheists have been seen to post comments on social media saying that 'if Jesus returns, they will kill Him again'. Many people across the world have replied to these posts expressing their same hatred of Jesus.

7. **Identity delusion:** We are now seeing the delusion that 'men can menstruate and can give birth', when in fact the truth is that these 'men' are actually women who have chosen to change their identity to that of a man. They may have had hormone treatment and surgery to make themselves appear masculine, but a simple DNA test will prove that their chromosomes are still that of a female. Nothing can alter their created, biological identity. Yes, women who have changed their *outward identity* to appear as a male, can menstruate and give birth; but that is because their body is still that of a female, even though they now look like a man. This does not translate to the deception being promoted that 'men can menstruate and give birth'. No biological male can ever do either. It is against God's created order. This is the biological and scientific truth, even though many may not like it or accept it.

Dr. Paul McHugh, former psychiatrist in chief at The Johns Hopkins Hospital, and author of *Try to Remember:*

Psychiatry's Clash Over Meaning, Memory, and Mind, wrote an article for *Courage International, Inc.* in which he said:

> "'Sex change' is biologically impossible. People who undergo sex-reassignment surgery do not change from men to women or vice versa. Rather, they become feminized men or masculinized women.'

(Link: https://couragerc.org/wp-content/uploads/2018/02/TransgenderSurgery.pdf)

8. **Terrorist activity:** There has been a rapid rise in terrorist attacks by groups and individual people, ranging from knife crime to widespread bombings. In the past year or so, Sweden has experienced over 100 incidents of gang-related explosions; something that is new to that nation. Not a day goes by without a terrorist incident being reported somewhere around the world.

9. **Social media bullying:** Social media has always been a hotbed for bullying and hostility, but since the turn of 2020, much of it has turned into intense hatred that can only be described as demonic, with people (and their families) being threatened with rape and murder for simply sharing views that are different to the views that others hold.

10. **Global civil unrest and commotion:** God's Word instructs believers to love all people. This is because He created every human being, and as such, *every life* matters to Him. But love does not remain silent in the face of the misuse of power, especially when it is used to bring destruction. To remain silent and just allow something to happen is to condone that behaviour. In a culture that demands that we 'love' everyone, we have to examine what love truly looks like according to the One who created us. God's love for the whole human race is merciful, forgiving and restoring, but His love also requires the revealing and correcting of anything that it contrary to

His Word, in ourselves and also in society in general. It is not unloving to do this, although it is often received as such. Nevertheless, as the time hastens towards the return of the Lord, God is exposing these things in such dramatic ways that it can feel quite terrifying watching them unfold. What I am about to write is an example of the destruction that can manifest when those who feel aggrieved demand that the present-day society repays them for historical injustices perpetrated against their ancestors from many centuries ago.

Following the tragic death of George Floyd whilst being arrested by the police, (although he was known to be involved in criminal activity and drug use), the world has become engulfed in the rage of the Black Lives Matter protests and riots. The BLM movement is an organization shown on *wikipedia.org* to be supported by George Soros. By 'supported' we can assume this means financially. These riots have led to a great deal of destruction in many towns and cities around the world, the setting fire of law enforcement buildings, and demanding white people give up their homes and let black people live in them. Rioters have desecrated historical and Christian statues and monuments with BLM and ANTIFA graffiti emblazoned on them, and statues of Jesus have been decapitated. Added to this, there has been a huge rise in destruction and vandalism of churches, cathedrals and synagogues across the world. Many have been set on fire and others sprayed with satanic and Nazi symbols. The most recent hatred against Christianity is the burning of Bibles, with the perpetrators posting a video of this sacrilege on social media. There has also been an increase in the desecration of the gravestones of people's loved ones. All this from an organization which is allegedly *"a decentralized movement advocating for **non-violent** civil disobedience..."* (Author's emphasis)

(Link: https://en.wikipedia.org/wiki/Black_Lives_Matter)

Right in the early stages of the Covid19 lockdown in the United Kingdom, the BLM movement decided to ignore government instructions and hold protest marches in various cities and towns. One such protest took place in London at the site of The Cenotaph, the United Kingdom's monument to those who have given their lives in war, for *our* freedom. These protesters set fire to the Union Jack flag and desecrated the monument with graffiti.

The root of this lawlessness appears to be driven by a victimhood mentality that demands everyone accept their agenda, and if we refuse to comply, we will be attacked by them in some form or another. A young woman was murdered by BLM protesters for declaring that 'All Lives Matter'. While all this atrocity is going on, the police stand by and let it all happen. In some incidents, the police have actually run away in fear, when their job is to enforce the law on anyone who is perpetrating a crime or behaving in an anti-social manner, whatever their colour or race.

A spirit of *entitlement* dominates the heart of the movement, demanding that today's generation repays them for the actions of previous generations. Even when people today attempt to make efforts to ask for forgiveness for the sins of past generations, those involved in the riots do not seem satisfied with any moves of repentance or reparation. They seem fuelled by a deep hatred of anyone or anything that is contrary to their ideology. Many observers believe that this is a liberal, Marxist, anarchist movement which refuses to recognize authority and craves for 'freedom of the individual' regardless of the cost to the rest of society. If the actions of their supporters during protests is anything to go by, this may well be true. Yet in its manifesto on their website www.blacklivesmatter.com, it states;

"We intentionally build and nurture a beloved

community that is bonded together through a **beautiful struggle** that is restorative, **not depleting.**" (Author's emphasis)

Further, it states;

"To love and desire freedom and justice for ourselves **is a prerequisite for wanting the same for others.**" (Author's emphasis)

Such statements seem totally at odds with the violent, destructive actions that are being witnessed during their public protests, resulting in police officers being injured or killed. If wanting love, freedom and justice for themselves and also "wanting the same for others" is truly the BLM goal, what they are displaying during their protests seems to refute their claim. Rather than protesting in a truly peaceful manner to achieve the claims of their loving, free and just ideology, they seem completely unappeasable.

11. **Defunding the police:** The BLM movement is the driving force behind the push to 'Defund the Police'. They want to remove long-established law and order from society so that they can be 'free'. The result of their attempts to do this has seen horrific escalating lawlessness, with citizens screaming for the police to return to their jobs! When society removes those who uphold the law, the utopia of freedom which they desire never materializes; all that happens is that lawlessness increases.

12. **Mainstream support for BLM:** Big companies and organizations, including sporting events, are supporting the BLM movement and 'bowing the knee' in support of this Marxist organization, with some putting the BLM logo on their sports kit and stadium billboards. One wonders if they have ever taken the time to read the BLM manifesto, or if their motivation for jumping on this politically correct bandwagon is a 'woke' opportunity for 'virtue-signalling'.

13. **The institutional church and BLM:** With the institutional church now embracing anything that *seems* like a good idea, unsurprisingly, many of its leaders - including the archbishops - have fallen for the outwardly promoted deception of the BLM movement, without 'checking the label on the tin'. The Archbishop of Canterbury has stated that the Church needs to repent of its 'whiteness' and for displaying Jesus as being 'white'. He feels the need to assess every statue and monument around Westminster Cathedral (and probably others) with a view to removing them if they hold even a hint of history that might offend BLM protestors. Equally unsurprisingly, the newly appointed Archbishop of York seems to be clinging on to the Archbishop of Canterbury's coat tails. Meanwhile, to show its own support for BLM, St Albans Cathedral decided to replace the altarpiece painting of the nativity with a painting of the Last Supper depicting Jesus as a black man. Let's check our facts here; Jesus was a Jew, so if the Cathedral really wants to be biblically correct in its depicting of Jesus, it should ensure that He is portrayed as a Jew.

14. **The mantra of 'white supremacy':** The rise of 'white supremacy' accusations is mind-boggling. Not only do we see people of colour banging this drum, but even white people are demanding the removal of titles, names, and plaques of historical people, which they think may cause offence; wanting to change labels on products that have the word 'white' or 'whitening' on them, claiming that they are offensive and racist to anyone who is not white. Also, people who are white are now saying that they regret being white and want to repent of it; and I have seen evidence of church leaders standing up and renouncing and repenting of the colour that God created them! The same insanity is happening with the word 'Master'. There is a push to remove this word because the 'woke' culture says that it implies being dominated or controlled by a male.

15. **Political correctness:** The root of this agenda is the removal of freedom of speech, silencing those who hold contrary thoughts to the narrative of the so-called 'woke elite'. The 'woke' brigade vociferously 'guilt' those who refuse to go along with the twisted, intolerant views of political correctness, and they target them like a voodoo doll, often hounding them, even unto death.

16. **The 'thought police':** The police have now taken it upon themselves to analyse and scrutinize our thoughts, and interrogate us for the views that we hold, in case our beliefs could be deemed as offensive to others. Our thoughts can be reported as a 'hate crime' even if no crime has been committed. Just sharing our personal thoughts can result in a criminal record. In a country where freedom of speech is still the law, it would seem that the police appear to be acting contrary to the law by attempting to criminalize people for their own personal beliefs and opinions. (see www.faircop.org.uk)

17. **Delusion:** It seems we have entered the period of 'strong delusion'. Someone posted on social media, "Many say there will be a great awakening, the Bible says there will be strong delusion. People say there will be a great revival, Jesus says there will be a great falling away from the faith. Take heed that no one deceives you."

How true this is! I hope the examples I have listed above show a clear indication that society has been overtaken by a spirit of delusion, on a global scale. Thirty years ago, we would never have imagined that what we are now witnessing would ever occur. Yet here we are…

God's Word sums this up for us;

> "But understand this, that in the last days there will come times of difficulty. For people will be lovers of self, lovers of money, proud, arrogant, abusive,

disobedient to their parents, ungrateful, unholy, heartless, unappeasable, slanderous, without self-control, brutal, not loving good, treacherous, reckless, swollen with conceit, lovers of pleasure rather than lovers of God," – 2 Timothy 3:1-4 ESV

"Indeed, all who desire to live a godly life in Christ Jesus will be persecuted, **while evil people and impostors will go on from bad to worse, deceiving and being deceived.**" – 2 Timothy 3:12-13 ESV (Author's emphasis)

The above is a snapshot of the increase in lawlessness that is happening in 2020. I am sure there will be many other examples that could be added to the list by the time this book goes to print.

The Gospel to reach all Nations

Now, returning to the Matthew chapter 24 passage which we have been working through, next Jesus gives us the reassurance that if we bear up under all this suffering and hold on until the end, we will be saved, and during this time of the birth pains, the Gospel will be preached throughout the whole world as a testimony to all nations. We are living in the age where rapid growth in technology has made it possible to preach the Gospel to all corners of the earth. Using the internet, we can connect with people in other countries from the comfort of our own homes, or even when we are on the go, through our mobile phones. We can post a Holy Spirit empowered message on Twitter, Facebook or other social media platforms that could bring someone, even many, to Christ.

With the whole world in varying degrees of lockdown due to Covid19, the doors of most church buildings being still firmly closed even after a measure of lockdown easing, and 'mask-free' services not being conducted until governments decide that the virus has gone, now more than ever, the internet is being used to get the Gospel to the ends of the earth! Churches have turned to online livestreaming of their weekly services, and millions of people are logging in to watch and participate from their homes. Churches that only ever had a handful of people sitting in the pews are now seeing hundreds, and even thousands, 'attend' these livestreamed services. People are hungering and thirsting for God and for truth and are turning to Christ in their droves.

Jesus said that when the Gospel is preached to all nations, *then* 'the end' will come! What does He mean by this? When we read the start of the next section of Jesus' End Times sermon in Matthew 24:15-31 (which we will look at shortly) we will see that a marked change occurs upon the earth. It moves from what the world has experienced as the End Times birth pains (sent to us as God's final effort - during His period of grace - to wake up the world to repent and turn to Christ), to perilous times of immense suffering, oppression and calamity, the likes of which this world has never seen. This is what we know to be the start of the Great Tribulation, and it is the commencement of this period that Jesus is referring to when He says, "...*and then the end will come*." It is the final part of the End Times which will culminate in the Second Coming of Christ. We will look at all this shortly, under the sub-heading 'The Great Tribulation'.

Although what I am about to say next is not mentioned in Jesus' discourse in Matthew 24, a vision of it is given to the Apostle John by Jesus' angel in the Book of Revelation chapter 7. But I want to give you a quick glimpse of it so that you will be ready to study it when we look at the subject of the Rapture in more detail in the next chapter **'What will happen to the Church? – The Rapture of Believers'.**

Here is our quick glimpse: Just *before* the unimaginable horror of the Great Tribulation begins, two events occur which I believe are simultaneous with the start of the outpouring of God's wrath. These events are (a) the sealing of the 144,000 from the twelve tribes of Israel who will witness for Christ during the Great Tribulation, and

(b) the Rapture of the Church; the worldwide body of the faithful, repentant and obedient followers of Christ. I will give a more in-depth study of this in the next chapter.

But now we will continue with Jesus' message in Matthew chapter 24, where He takes us straight to the second part of the End Times, which most Christians describe as the Great Tribulation. We will read the biblical text shortly.

The Great Tribulation

After the faithful Bride of Christ has been taken up by Jesus into heaven, amongst the unbelievers who have been left behind on the earth, there will be people left who professed to be followers of Christ, but who lived their Christian lives like the five *unwise* virgins who were not keeping watch for the signs of the times, thus failing to ensure their readiness for Jesus' return for them. They will not be taken by the Bridegroom but will be left behind on the earth, and He will not allow them entry into the marriage of the Bridegroom with His Bride (see the Parable of the Ten Virgins, in Matthew 25). They will be left in the world to endure all that will come upon the earth in the Great Tribulation. When this period is finished, when Jesus finally returns at His Second Coming, unless they repent during the Great Tribulation, they will mourn at His appearing; mourning because of their rejection and rebellion of Him whilst they lived their lives on this earth; living as if His Word was something that they could mess around with, deceiving themselves that He would never ever return.

So, with the Bride of Christ having been taken out of the earth, let's see what will happen *after* the Rapture.

Antichrist Arising

We will now look at the Great Tribulation text in Matthew chapter 24:15-31 from the Amplified Bible translation. The very first thing that Jesus tells us about is the appearing of the Antichrist, described in the passage as *the abomination of desolation,* who stands in the Holy Place. I will talk about the Holy Place in a separate sub-heading further on.

The Antichrist's appearing will trigger the Great Tribulation; a time of great anguish which will come upon the earth; the final period leading up to Christ's Second Coming. I will let this passage speak for itself.

> "So when you see the ABOMINATION OF DESOLATION [the appalling sacrilege that astonishes and makes desolate], spoken of by the prophet Daniel, standing in the Holy Place (let the reader understand), then let those who are in Judea flee to the mountains [for refuge]. Whoever is on the housetop must not go down to get the things that are in his house [because there will not be enough time]. Whoever is in the field must not turn back to get his coat. And woe to those who are pregnant and to those who are nursing babies in those days! Pray that your flight [from persecution and suffering] will not be in winter, or on a Sabbath [when Jewish laws prohibit travel]. For at that time there will be a great tribulation (pressure, distress, oppression), such as has not occurred since the beginning of the world until now, nor ever will [again]. And if those days [of tribulation] had not been cut short, no human life would be saved; but for the sake of the elect (God's chosen ones) those days will be shortened. Then if anyone says to you [during the great tribulation], 'Look! Here is the Christ,' or 'There He is,' do not believe it. For false Christs and false prophets will appear and they will provide great signs and wonders, so as to deceive, if possible, even the elect (God's chosen ones). Listen carefully, I have told you in advance. So if they say to you, 'Look! He is in the wilderness,' do not go out there, or, 'Look! He is in the inner rooms [of a house],' do not believe it. For just as the lightning comes from the east and flashes as far as the

west, so will be the coming [in glory] of the Son of Man [everyone will see Him clearly]. Wherever the corpse is, there the vultures will flock together.

"Immediately after the tribulation of those days THE SUN WILL BE DARKENED, AND THE MOON WILL NOT PROVIDE ITS LIGHT, AND THE STARS WILL FALL from the sky, and the powers of the heavens will be shaken. And at that time the sign of the Son of Man [coming in His glory] will appear in the sky, and then all the tribes of the earth [and especially Israel] will mourn [regretting their rebellion and rejection of the Messiah], and they will see the SON OF MAN COMING ON THE CLOUDS OF HEAVEN with power and great glory [in brilliance and splendor]. **And He will send His angels with A LOUD TRUMPET and THEY WILL GATHER TOGETHER His elect (God's chosen ones) from the four winds, from one end of the heavens to the other.**" (Author's emphasis)

Just a note: I have highlighted that last verse to point out that the gathering referred to in this passage is *not* the Rapture of believers from the earth; it is the gathering together, from one end of the heavens to the other, of all the raptured believers who are already in heaven, who will return with Jesus to earth to rule and reign with Him for one-thousand years (see Revelation 19).

The Rapture of the Church will signify the commencement of the *final* 3½ year period of the Great Tribulation with the Antichrist being fully revealed, as described in the above passage. However, this person will already be on the earth *prior* to the Rapture, but in his disguise as 'the saviour' of a world in total chaos. He will be the world's global leader marked by the signing a 7-year peace treaty with Israel, described as a covenant with 'many' (see Daniel 9:27), which we saw in Chapter 2. For the initial 3½ years of his rule, he will be hailed as the best thing this world has ever seen. Using his powers of deception, he will arise to bring *his* 'solution' to the world's chaos and will restore peace to the world for a period of 3½ years.

Many believers and Bible scholars have varying views on this subject. After much prayer and many years of looking at this myself, with a deep longing to understand, I have come to the conclusion that, prior to the Rapture, believers will see this man arise in his 'saviour' role, and will witness the covenant being signed by Israel and the 'many' (many nations). Believers will know that 3½ years after this signing, this worldly 'saviour' will be revealed as the Antichrist. At this point of the revealing of the Antichrist, the Lord will Rapture the Bride of Christ from the earth. Almost simultaneously with the disappearance of the Church, and whilst the world is rejoicing in its new-found period of 'peace and safety', sudden destruction will come upon them, and they will not escape (see 1 Thessalonians 5:1-3). This man in whom this world will put all its faith and trust, will completely change from being the global 'saviour' to being a global tyrant. The Antichrist will be revealed for the whole world to see, and will ensconce himself in the new Jewish temple in Jerusalem, setting himself up as 'God'. Then will commence the final period of 3½ years, which is the time of the Great Tribulation.

As I mentioned in Chapter 2, it is interesting that the world has just witnessed the historic signing of the *Abraham Accord* peace treaty between Israel, the United Arab Emirates and Bahrain. This was brokered by President Donald Trump and was made possible by the efforts of Crown Prince Sheikh Mohamed bin Zayed of the UAE. But rather disturbingly, part of the deal is that Israel agrees to the establishment of a Palestinian state by an exchange of territories. Basically, Israel has agreed to give some of its land to secure peace with its neighbours. We need to realize how serious this is. God gave the Jews the land of Israel as their inheritance in a binding, everlasting covenant (see Psalm 105:8-11). Dividing their inheritance for the sake of peace must surely have consequences.

We are living in the most eye-opening period of world history. End

Times Bible prophecy is unfolding before our eyes, and the 'great cloud of witnesses' that have gone before us into heaven, plus all of the heavenly host must be looking over the ramparts of heaven, watching things unfold and waiting with longing for the arrival of the Bride of Christ.

As we saw earlier in this book, in Chapter 2, and also confirmed by Jesus in the Matthew 24:15-31 passage a few pages previously, the angel of the Lord gave a vision to Daniel of the End Times, the arising of the Antichrist, and the Great Tribulation. We will study the Antichrist's full role in the Great Tribulation later in Chapter 6.

Returning again to Matthew 24:15-31, as we can see from what Jesus is telling believers in His End Times discourse, horrendous times will come upon the earth, and even more false christs and false prophets will arise to deceive the immensely distressed inhabitants of the earth. He then finishes His message by describing the time of the Great Tribulation period. Great signs will appear in the heavens, the sun will go dark, and the moon will no longer give any light. The stars will fall from the sky and the very powers of heaven will be shaken. Jesus says He will then appear, coming on the clouds in the sky with great power and glory, and all humanity (especially the unbelieving in Israel) will mourn that they rebelled and rejected Him. He will send His angels with a loud trumpet sound to gather His chosen ones from one end of the heavens to the other to rule and reign with Him (which I referred to earlier).

Moving on to verses 32-39, Jesus then gives us something to think about and to make sure we are ready for.

> "Now learn this lesson from the fig tree: As soon as its young shoots become tender and it puts out its leaves, you know that summer is near; so you, too, when you see all these things [taking place], know for certain that He is near, right at the door. I assure you and most solemnly say to you, this generation [the people living when these signs and events begin] will not pass away until all these

things take place. Heaven and earth [as now known] will pass away, but My words will not pass away.

But of that [exact] day and hour no one knows, not even the angels of heaven, nor the Son [in His humanity], but the Father alone. For the coming of the Son of Man (the Messiah) will be just like the days of Noah. For as in those days before the flood they were eating and drinking, marrying and giving in marriage, until the [very] day when Noah entered the ark, and they did not know or understand until the flood came and swept them all away; so will the coming of the Son of Man be [unexpected judgment]." – Matthew 24:32-39 AMP

There is something I want to pick up on in this passage. It is the verse where Jesus says,

"I assure you and most solemnly say to you, this generation [the people living when these signs and events begin] will not pass away until all these things take place."

This is very important, but it can be easily missed. Jesus is saying very clearly that the generation of people who are living at the time when all these signs of the End Times *begin* to happen, will *not* pass away. To establish which generation He is referring to, we have to determine at what point the 'birth pain' signs and events began to escalate. As I mentioned earlier, they began in earnest when the nation of Israel was reborn on 14th May 1948, and her people began to return from their places of exile around the world, where they have lived since 70 AD. As of 2020, with the global Covid19 outbreak, national leaders are calling all their people, wherever they live in the world, back to their birth nations for their safety. *This includes Israel.* Soon, it is possible that all Jews will be back in their homeland of Israel; the land promised to them and given to them by God.

"And I will establish my covenant between me and you

and your offspring after you throughout their generations for an everlasting covenant, to be God to you and to your offspring after you. And I will give to you and to your offspring after you the land of your sojournings, all the land of Canaan, for an everlasting possession, and I will be their God." – Genesis 17:7-8 ESV

'He is the LORD our God;
his judgments are in all the earth.
He remembers his covenant forever,
the word that he commanded, for a thousand generations,
the covenant that he made with Abraham,
his sworn promise to Isaac,
which he confirmed to Jacob as a statute,
to Israel as an everlasting covenant,
saying, "To you I will give the land of Canaan
as your portion for an inheritance."' – Psalm 105:7-11 ESV

The date of 14th May 1948 is the trigger that began the *increase* in End Times birth pain events.

All those born from 14th May 1948 onwards belong to the final generation that Jesus is talking about. How do we establish the period of a 'generation'? Biblically speaking, God's Word in Psalm 90:10 says that the life of a person is three-score years and ten (70 years), or if they have strength, maybe four-score years (80 years). If we take a generation to be 70 years, and apply that to the year 1948, it takes us to 2018 (which has now passed). If we take a generation to be 80 years, it takes us to the year 2028. Just to reassure you, I am absolutely *not* a 'date-setter'! I am simply showing you what Jesus has said, and applying God's 'generation' calculator to merely offer a thought that, if Jesus has said that the generation that sees these End Times things begin to happen will *not* pass away before His return, then by God's own Word, the return of the Lord could occur between 2018 and 2028. I am writing this in 2020. I reiterate that I do not know when it will be, nor does anyone else (see Matthew

25:13). All I know is that Jesus exhorts us to be watchful of the signs of the times, and to be ready and alert for His sudden appearing.

Jesus finishes His End Times discourse in verses 32-39 by telling us that despite all that is occurring on the earth, the people of the world will carry on in their normal manner, eating, drinking and marrying, and having an attitude that 'everything will be alright'. Humanity will carry on in this complacent manner right up to the time of Jesus' Second Coming; the same as in the time of Noah, until the flood came and destroyed all of civilization, except Noah and his family, and the ark full of animals.

In the following quote, over 100 years ago, J.C. Ryle was writing about the effects upon the world at the sudden return of Christ. When we look at the chaos in the world today, and the sudden shock that people are feeling because of the effects that lockdown measures are having upon their lives, Ryle's words describe perfectly what humanity is experiencing today with the sudden stoppage of all that we have known. He is right that the world is caught up in itself and totally unprepared for Jesus' coming.

> 'Think for a moment how little the world is prepared for such an event. Look at the towns and cities of the earth, and think of them. Mark how most men are entirely absorbed in the things of time, and utterly engrossed with the business of their calling. Banks, counting-houses, shops, politics, law, medicine, commerce, railways, banquets, balls, theatres, each and all are drinking up the hearts and souls of thousands, and thrusting out the things of God. Think what a fearful shock the sudden stoppage of all these things would be, the sudden stoppage which will be in the day of Christ's appearing. If only one great house of business stops payment now, it makes a great sensation. What then shall be the crash when the whole machine of worldly affairs shall stand still at once?' [2]

Section C – What's coming next?

The Holy Place

In Section B, in the passage of Matthew 24:15-31, Jesus referred to the abomination that causes desolation (the Antichrist) standing in the Holy Place. The temple in Jerusalem was destroyed in 70 AD and has never been rebuilt to this day. But in order for the Antichrist to stand in the Holy Place and proclaim himself to be God (see 2 Thessalonians 2:3-5) and to put an end to the sacrifices (see Daniel 9:27) a new Jewish temple must be built where the Jewish sacrificial system will be operating again. Also, in John's vision of the End Times 7-year Tribulation period, the angel told him to measure the temple and the altar (See Revelation 11:1-2). Therefore, it is clear that a new temple will be in existence during the Tribulation.

In recent years, this has been the subject of much discussion. There are many websites containing great detail on the rebuilding of the third temple. Those involved in this project say that they have discovered many temple artefacts hidden in the ancient city underneath Jerusalem, and that they have been recreating all the official items that would be used in the temple ceremonies, including training the Levite priests in animal sacrifice. They say that everything is 'ready to go' the moment those in authority give them the official go-ahead to start the rebuilding.

For a fascinating book on this, I recommend reading *The New Temple and the Second Coming* by Grant R. Jeffrey.

It is possible, even highly likely, that the global leader will be the one who will agree for this third temple to be built, and it will be in full use by the Levitical priests at the time that this man is suddenly revealed to be the Antichrist. This will bring about the fulfilment of Bible prophecy where he will then stand in the Holy Place and set himself up as 'God'. We may begin to see the rebuilding of the new temple prior to the Rapture of the Church.

Another interesting fact is that in 2018, Israel produced the 'New Temple Coin' to commemorate 70 years of independence. On one side is an engraved image of the temple, and on the reverse is an engraving of two heads; one being of King Cyrus, and the other being of President Donald Trump. I will not make any further comment on this.

Let's now move on to the subject of the New World Order, the One World Religion, and the cashless society which will be set up by the global leader, who will become the Antichrist.

The New World Order and the One World Religion

As I mentioned in the Introduction of this book, a time is fast approaching where this world will be under the control of a global government with a global religion, ruled by a leader who will eventually materialize as the Antichrist. Chapters 13 and 17 of the Book of Revelation indicate this, which we will study in Chapter 6.

Many church leaders are not teaching the flock about the End Times or Bible prophecy, and as such, vast swathes of Christians have barely any knowledge of future events from God's Word. Some think the New World Order is some far-fetched, unrealistic ideology that will never happen. Others believe it to be merely a conspiracy theory. This complacency is deeply disturbing. What is written in God's Word is going to be fulfilled at some point. A quick search on the internet and social media will reveal a raft of information concerning the subject of this section.

Rather than remain closed-minded on this, my own search revealed that it is the Vatican's desire to create a New World Order with a One World Religion as the way forward for the 21st century, for the purpose of 'religious unity' and 'world unity and peace'. Meetings have been conducted over the years, with many world leaders and heads of religious institutions and spiritual organisations in attendance; the latest major educational event being held on 14th May 2020, with the Pope's aim to advance his One World Religion vision. Very disturbingly, these events include high-profile Christian church leaders from many of the major denominations. The articles suggest that the meetings hope to persuade these leaders, from all forms of 'faith', to embrace the ideology of this New World Order and One World Religion. With the occasional media reports of these meetings, and the spin that is put on them to bring 'peace and security' to the global population, at some point it would then be easy to put their ideology into effect. In my research, I found that some European countries report that between 70-90% of their young people, aged 16-29, describe themselves as non-religious. We are now living in the era of 21st century post-Christian 'freedom'; a situation that is ripe for exploitation by a global figure with designs on world domination presented under the guise of unity and world peace, and using the Christian-speak of *'loving thy neighbour as thyself'* to persuade all to follow where this global 'pied-piper' leads them.

There is information that religious leaders plan to merge Christianity and Islam, creating a 'unified' One World Religion called 'Chrislam'. Many Christians have not heard of this, but in fact it is not a new idea. It first came into being in Lagos in the 1980's by a man called Tela Tella, who claimed that an angel of God told him to mix both of these religions to bring peace between them. For two interesting articles on this, visit www.eaec.org, *The Unholy Union of Christianity & Islam*, and also www.thirdmill.org, *What is Chrislam?*

Although not much has been heard about this over the past 40 years, no doubt those in high places will have been working on it behind closed doors. Only now does it appear to be coming to fruition. There is a dedicated website, www.chrislam.org which states that this current interfaith group is known as the *Islamic-Christian Dialogue Committee*. There are many other websites discussing this subject, so it is not something that is imaginary or a conspiracy theory. In fact, I stumbled upon a site (or was it the hand of God?) which states that Berlin is to build the first

'Chrislam Church', called *The House of One*, which will be an all-in-one mosque, church and synagogue, where Muslims, Christians and Jews can come together to worship and pray, albeit in separate designated areas. Their website is www.house-of-one.org

If it truly is their intention to merge these major religions into one global religion, I felt that there must be some sort of planned date for this. As I continued reading their website, I discovered that they had planned to conduct their 'Foundation Stone Ceremony' on 14th April 2020, but due to the Covid19 pandemic, that ceremony was postponed. All I can think is that this must be by God's divine intervention!

Discovering that piece of information was a shock! The reality dawned on me that possibly 99.99% of Christians would have no idea of this website or what is going on. Many simply cannot believe that those at the top of Church hierarchy could be involved in such things.

In addition to this, as recently as January 2020, meetings were held at the Pontifical Gregorian University in Rome to discuss what is known as the *Abrahamic Faiths Initiative*, which effectively is the Chrislam One World Religion under a more 'acceptable' name. A group of twenty-five Jewish, Muslim and Christian world leaders attended this event. The U.S Ambassador to the Holy See, Callista Gingrich said,

> "The Abrahamic Faiths Initiative serves as a powerful demonstration that, through fraternity, cooperation, and mutual respect between the Abrahamic faiths, peace in our world is possible."
>
> (Link: https://www.andrewbostom.org/2020/02/the-abrahamic-faiths-initiative-is-submission-to-islam/)

The initiative was signed by Pope Francis and the Grand Imam of Al-Azhar, with the help of Crown Prince Mohamed bin Zayed of the UAE.

For more information of the Crown Prince's involvement in both the *Abrahamic Faiths Initiative* (Chrislam) document signing and also President Trump's *Abraham Accord* peace treaty between Israel, the UAE and Bahrain, visit;

https://www.nowtheendbegins.com/chrislam-abraham-accord-between-israel-uae-was-missing-link-needed-to-launch-pope-francis-abrahamic-faiths-initiative/

One way or another, world and religious leaders are intent on moving forward with their plan for a One World Religion. This lines up with Bible prophecy. This End Times event of the New World Order and the One World Religion is being fulfilled in our lifetime, and as followers of Christ, we need to study God's Word on this subject, keep our eyes and ears alert to the signs of the times on the earth, and remain steadfast in our faith when the pressure intensifies, coercing us to compromise and conform for the sake of 'religious coexistence'.

Right from the start of this pandemic there has been the call for a global government, a global currency and a global religion, with national leaders making their plan very visible to the watching world. No longer are their intentions hidden behind the closed doors of their offices of power. Their intentions are now making headline news! No longer is it just some far-off future ideology that will affect future generations long after we have died. It is a 'full in the face' reality, possibly being put into full effect in our own lifetime.

So, we will now look at how the Covid19 outbreak fits in with the plan for this New World Order. We will start with something that the media has been subtly priming us with for several years.

The Cashless Society

Internet searches reveal that those who are the driving force for the New World Order, desire to create a global digital currency and get rid of cash altogether; what many are calling a 'cashless society', with all financial transactions being made through technology contained in a microchip device inserted in our hand. This technology, originally known as the RFID chip, has been in production for some years, and the early version of it now exists and is being implemented in various countries, promoted as being used for 'safety' or 'security'. But in order to create a world where cash no longer exists, something has got to happen to make the global population so fearful of handling cash, they will eagerly accept an alternative way of making payments.

Prior to any mention of such technology being used in humans, the idea of future digital microchips has been drip-fed into our subconsciousness for many years. We all know that pets have progressed from having a metal tag attached to their collar containing the name of the owner and a telephone number. But now our pets, and even commercial livestock are required to have some sort of microchip under their skin for tracking purposes, and containing their medical data. At first, we probably thought this was a great idea, little realising that this could be the first step on the ladder towards getting us to consider having something like this for ourselves.

Initially advertised as the best way to keep a track on the whereabouts of children and other vulnerable people, such as the elderly, to 'keep them safe', other articles suggest that at some point, we will all have this device, primarily containing our medical information, but in due time, including all our financial information so that we can 'do business' with the swipe of our hand over a digital payment device.

We are already halfway there with this with the use of contactless cards at the checkout, as well as the facility of paying for goods on our mobile phones. There are even reports that some businesses are requiring their staff to have a microchip implanted in the back of their hand for identification purposes, and to access their work premises easily by waving their hand across a security scanner.

If all this sounds horrifying, well it should do! This sounds very much like a gradual build up to the 'Mark of the Beast' mentioned in the Book of Revelation (see Revelation 13:16-18), where no one will be able to buy or sell anything unless they have this 'mark' on their right hand or on their forehead.

Several books have been written on the subject of the Mark of the Beast and the Cashless Society; *The End of Money* and *Cashless*, both by Mark Hitchcock, are just two of them. Also, *Trumpet Blast Warning* by Jason Carter, has a chapter on the Mark of the Beast.

In a world of ever-increasing technology, it is a constant temptation to have the latest 'gadget'. Many of the younger generation, even those in the Church, seem to think it is 'cool' to have a world where cash is no longer needed. They do not seem to realise that each gadget that is advertised as the latest new thing in 'technological progress', is a step nearer to the mandatory insertion of the microchip into our hand.

The arrival of Covid19 has created the perfect situation for governments and the media to promote the fear that is required to do away with cash. Heavily 'suggesting' that the virus can survive on cash for up to 10 days, and be transferred from person to person, our national leaders and the media brain-wash the population into believing that everyone's life will be put at risk of contracting it and we could all die. The eventual outcome will be an inserted digital device that will eradicate the use of cash forever.

Let's look at this whole issue because it all leads to the setting up of the End Times prophecy of global control.

Section D – Global control

World leaders and the media have spent many months feeding us with large doses of fear in their ploy to get us to believe that the Covid19 virus is a pandemic which they *need* to keep track of in order to keep people safe and, if necessary, lockdown whole nations again if it rears its ugly head in the slightest. I will simply comment that the recorded numbers of deaths *from* the virus are being investigated, particularly in the United Kingdom, due to the fact that deaths by *other* causes are also being included in the Covid19 figures, even if the deceased did not have the virus but had been in contact with someone who did. This has led to over-inflated death figures, fuelling the label of a 'pandemic' when many scientists are now saying it is nothing of the sort. With the current scandal surrounding the false-positive test results, the true figure of genuine cases of Covid19 is believed by many to be significantly lower than what is being reported by the UK Government. The following link explains this;

https://www.youtube.com/watch?v=06yja21V7xg

We should be asking ourselves why, to date, the Government has not been reporting the correct statistics. If this is happening in the United Kingdom, one can imagine that this same scenario may well be occurring in other countries.

How did Covid19 appear?

I referred to this in the Introduction of this book. Many think the virus is simply a variant and more severe form of the common flu virus, but for a virus like this to just 'suddenly appear' is not normal. According to at least two renowned virologists (Dr Judy Mikovitz and Dr Li-Meng Yan) it is impossible for Covid19 to have developed naturally; it could only have been created in a laboratory. This has led to speculation that Covid19 was being created and tested as a potential bioweapon in a laboratory in Wuhan, China and somehow it 'escaped' in Dec 2019, with authorities keeping the outbreak quiet for weeks, hoping to contain its spread. Meanwhile, many people travelled to and from China to other countries around the world, taking the virus with them.

Many believe the intention behind unleashing a bioweapon is

to bring about a pandemic that will shut down the world almost instantly, crippling the global economy to such a degree that it will *need* a global government and a global leader to come up with a plan to 'save' the world. As previously mentioned, humanity will be desperate for a solution to its distress... *any solution* that will enable them to return to some semblance of normality. A One World government headed by its powerful global leader will bring their solution to this problem, implementing a global currency to stabilize and reboot the world's catastrophic economic meltdown. The world's population will hail him as their 'saviour', worshipping him for saving them from their misery. In the run up to a global government, world leaders will get the reboot underway through the use of face masks. If we want to buy our food, we will be asked to wear a mask in the shops. At first it is recommended, but eventually it becomes mandatory, then enforceable by law. If we refuse to wear one, we basically cannot buy our food or conduct any business.

Face Mask Mania

Here in the United Kingdom, right from the start of the lockdown on 23rd March 2020, the subject of mask wearing has been one of total confusion. As I type this section in July 2020, after four months of no clear guidelines on the wearing of masks, and no enforcement to wear one, the Government has now imposed this upon us from 24th July. During the height of the death rates in April and May, people happily went to the supermarkets without masks, and during that time the death figures gradually reduced. Some people did wear a mask, but at that critical time of high death rates, most mask-wearers *did not* confront or verbally attack those who didn't wear one. However, I personally was accosted by a man wearing both a face mask and gloves, who accused me of potentially infecting him. This encounter left me deeply shaken.

However, the Government has now catapulted its citizens into a new dimension because of its inconsistent and indecisive approach to the issue of wearing a mask. With mandatory mask wearing now required in all shops and enclosed spaces, (with exemptions for people who have conditions that mean they will be in distress wearing a mask), those who go into a shop without a mask on for *valid* reasons are in fear of other shoppers staring at them, pointing the finger at them as if they have got leprosy and ought to have a label around their necks stating 'Unclean'. Some have had mask-wearers confronting them in a hostile manner, threatening to call the police. Even though the UK Government has made provision for these exemptions, still the mask-wearers seem to think it is their 'duty' to expose and shame anyone who hasn't got a mask on, egged on by comments made by the Commissioner of the Metropolitan Police Service. The Government has even produced an Exemption Card for people (like me) to hold up in people's faces if they challenge us. We shouldn't have to do this, yet the mindset of many over-zealous mask-wearers is that those who can't wear one should not even be allowed out of their houses!

What the Government has done by imposing mask wearing after months of freedom of choice on this matter, has caused a situation of immense division between the citizens of this country. People are beginning to hate each other based on the wearing or non-wearing of a mask. With deeply conflicting information as to whether a mask even protects us or others from the virus, in the United Kingdom we now find ourselves forced to muzzle-up or incur a £200 fine, increasing substantially for repeat non-compliance.

Our immune systems have been created by God to fight invasions by 'enemies'. The symptoms we experience when we are infected by a foreign body is the immune system's fighting response to the invasion. Over 99.9% of people who get ill will recover from the attack. But we have reached a stage where people are so full of fear that they don't know what to do. Rather than think for themselves, they only want to believe what they hear from so-called 'experts' on the TV news, much of which later on is shown to be faulty or misleading information. But having been duped by politicians and the media into a state of panic bordering on hysteria, it is very hard to persuade people that the fear they are experiencing is largely unfounded.

Having succeeded in their aim of creating fear in most of society, and using the face mask as an easy and convincing method of control to return to a relatively 'normal' way of life, the next level of control is the introduction of technology to track and trace our movements, ostensibly under the guise of tracking the movements of the virus.

Track and Trace Technology

The intention behind this system is that if someone has tested positive for Covid19, those whom they have been in contact with can be notified immediately, resulting in them having to self-isolate for 14 days to see if they come down with symptoms. But surely those people would have to notify everyone that they have also been in contact with to inform them that they may *potentially* have the virus which they may have potentially passed on to them! Working this through to its logical conclusion, almost everyone would constantly be receiving a notification on their phone that someone they know has either got the virus or has been in contact with someone who has. Everyone would find themselves repeatedly having to self-isolate, with the outcome that they could find themselves unemployed. This would grind nations to a halt even more than a temporary lockdown period. With this system not bringing the results that those in authority require, it will lead to the next level of control.

Vaccination and Digital ID

The information I am about to share is readily available in the public domain. In a sea full of misinformation, I would encourage you to do your own research in order to discern what is true and what is fake. In a world that has turned 'evil into good' and 'good into evil', we have reached the stage where it may seem impossible to discern anything fully. However, as I mentioned in the Introduction, our discernment must be based on whether what we see and hear lines up with what is written in the Word of God. If it doesn't line up, then we can safely dismiss it as a conspiracy theory. But if it does line up with prophecy, then our ears should prick up and cause us to pay attention. I am simply sharing what I feel may line up with what I see written in the Bible. You are free to have a different view, but as I have felt very strongly that the Lord gave me the task to write this book, I feel that I must at least get the very basic details down in print. What you personally choose to do with it is for you to decide. It is not my intention to influence you, but merely to share the information that is freely available in the public space.

Quantum Dot, ID2020 Technology and Google 'SkinMarks'

Using the media to promote the global Covid19 virus as a 'pandemic', there is immense pressure by world governments to get the global population vaccinated. In the United Kingdom, the Government has recently secured access to 350 million vaccine doses. The total population is about 68 million. That means that there will be enough vaccines available to give each person 5 shots!

There is evidence that indicates that the manufacture of vaccines may involve using tissue from the cells of aborted babies;

> "The use of fetal tissue in vaccine development is the practice of researching, developing, and producing vaccines through the use of cultured (laboratory-grown) human fetal cells. The vaccines themselves contain none of the original cells and - if any - very slight traces of human DNA fragments."

> (Link: https://en.wikipedia.org/wiki/Use_of_fetal_tissue_in_vaccine_development).

The abortion industry is heavily promoted and heavily funded by organizations involved in the vaccine industry. This ought to sound alarm bells. Yet many close their eyes to this horrific information. They simply want to believe that compulsory vaccination would be a good idea, based on the promoted spin that it is just a simple vaccine designed to protect us. However there is a lot of information suggesting that a compulsory DNA-altering vaccine could contain a 'Nano-Dot' or 'Quantum Dot' dye (incorporating the enzyme 'Luciferase' with a patent number 060606) that is able to store medical history (particularly vaccination information) and this technology dye would be delivered under the skin at the same time as the vaccine is injected.

In July 2020, I found an article about a "Reddit 'Ask Me Anything' session" on 18th March 2020, where ex-founder of Microsoft, Bill Gates confirmed that he was working on this Quantum Dot implant, which will consist of a micron-scale capsule containing the dots that will hold our records. But interestingly, as I came to insert the link to this article (in September 2020), the reddit.com link to his comments shows that he removed this information. However, the information can be found in the following link:

https://principia-scientific.com/bill-gates-digital-tattoo-implant-to-track-covid-19-vaccine-compliance/

In a tweet posted on Twitter on 30th April 2020, Bill Gates said,

'Humankind has never had a more urgent task than creating broad immunity for coronavirus. It's going to require a global cooperative effort like this world has never seen. But I know we'll get it done. There's simply no alternative.'

https://twitter.com/BillGatesstatus/1255902245922709506?s=08

In a CBS News interview, Bill Gates indicated that multiple vaccines could be necessary to keep us protected against the virus, saying "None of the vaccines at this point appear like they'll work in a single dose."

(Link: https://www.cbsnews.com/news/coronavirus-vaccine-bill-gates-multiple-doses/).

None of this is a secret. His plan is to vaccinate the global population, not just once, but *repeatedly*.

At the same time, he is involved in the ID2020 Certification Mark. This will use the vaccination program as a platform for creating a digital identity, referred to in the quote below. As I mentioned regarding the future cashless society, with fear being generated that the Covid19 virus could survive on cash for up to 10 days, could this ID platform eventually be used to force the world to accept a digital currency where only those who have this digital technology under their skin will be able to engage fully in society; to do business and to buy or sell?

In an article posted on social media by citizentruth.org, dated 13th July 2020, its heading stated;

"A new biometric identity platform partnered with the Gates-funded GAVI vaccine alliance and Mastercard will launch in West Africa and combine COVID-19 vaccinations, cashless payments, and potential law enforcement applications."

This article stated that Mastercard describes itself as,

'a leader toward a "World Beyond Cash", and its partnership with GAVI marks a novel approach towards linking a biometric digital identity system, vaccination records, and a payment system into one single cohesive platform.'

(Link: https://citizentruth.org/africa-to-become-testing-ground-for-trust-stamp-vaccine-record-and-payment-system/).

The article on the citizentruth.org site is a real eye-opener of the power, money and influence that is being thrown into the desire of powerful, global influencers to have us all in their grip both physically and financially. From just the parts of the article that I have cited above, this sounds too much like the Mark of the Beast technology to merely be a coincidence.

And as if the above is not enough to prime the world to the idea of having something placed on or under our skin, the latest advance in technology which could replace our smartphones is the Google 'SkinMarks'.

(Link: https://research.google/pubs/pub46726/).

Using high-tech rub-on tattoos, these 'Skin Marks' could turn our bodies into a touchpad, with embedded sensors that can track the wearer's movements. The idea is that this is supposedly 'for fun', but once the idea catches on, it could very easily be used for sinister purposes. There is plenty of information about this on the internet, including some videos.

Many people who go to church each week have no idea what God's Word says on these issues because their church leaders remain silent on the subject, possibly because they think the subject of the Mark of the Beast is too difficult for them to explain to their congregations, or because they believe it is an outlandish fantasy story only suitable for making Hollywood movies. Both Revelation 13 and the Mark of the Beast are **God's Word!** Our church leaders should be warning believers, in the strongest possible terms, of what is written.

So, where is all this leading?

A Pandemic or a 'Plandemic'?

I am typing this section in September 2020. After 6 months of unrelenting media fearmongering regarding anything relating to Covid19, and with mounting evidence that all is *not* what it seems, we must surely wonder whether Covid19 is really a 'serious pandemic', and why it has been hyped up to such a level of suffocating hysteria, leaving vast numbers of people almost paralysed with fear that they worry they will drop dead the moment they walk out of their front door.

Thankfully, many courageous medical professionals are now rising up to take a stand against the political and media spin that is used to control society in the name of 'staying safe'. These brave people are breaking their silence because they know that something is not right, and they cannot remain silent any longer, as to do so would render them complicit in a deception. At the time of writing, many frontline medical staff have been sworn to silence by their employers, forcing them not to speak about what is actually going on in their hospitals, with Covid wards almost empty, staff with nothing to do, and many being furloughed or laid off altogether.

There have been reports on social media and YouTube videos of people sending Covid19 test kits back *unopened and unused* and then receiving a letter from their medical provider saying that their test was 'positive'! Some have used the test swab, not on themselves but on a piece of fruit or other non-human material. After labelling it as their own personal swab, they have sent it in for analysis and also received a 'positive' Covid19 test result. How can this be? What is going on?

A steady trickle of whistle-blowers are now daring to confront those who are in control of the information that is fed to society. These warriors for truth and justice are producing videos exposing the deception in order to get the truth out into the public space. Yet many of these videos are rapidly taken down by Google and YouTube. Why is this? Could it be because these organizations are part of the political/media collusion, and they don't want their dark deceptions being revealed by these whistle-blowing experts? Whistle-blowers have got nothing to gain when they expose what is going on. In fact, their courage puts them in danger of losing everything. This is why many believe that when these big organizations remove expository videos from the public space, it is a sign that a deception is taking place.

Many data analysts have suggested that the Covid19 figures for the United Kingdom (for August 2020) indicated that approximately 99.94% of the population have either not had the virus, or within this figure, those who have had it have survived, mostly without hospital treatment. A figure of 0.05% have died *with* the virus, and 0.01% died *of* the virus. Similar percentages have been reported in other nations. Statistics like this do not indicate that this virus is a pandemic. So, the question needs to be asked; why have world governments made the devastating decision to impose a global lockdown knowing full well that such prolonged action will result in catastrophic social and economic consequences? It is clearly not because they simply want us to 'stay safe'. No government would crash its nation's economy as a gesture of its 'care' towards its citizens! The way the crisis is being handled globally would indicate that it is being used for purposes *unrelated* to the virus.

Yet, many people still label such thoughts or possibilities as a 'conspiracy theory'. They scoff at the suggestion that world governments and their various partners could be involved in some sort of plan to use a potential crisis to control humanity. It may well be just a theory, but we surely need to investigate the possibility that it could be true. As human beings, we have a tendency to unquestioningly believe and trust politically-appointed 'experts' who say they have got our best welfare at heart and wouldn't dream of doing such a thing to humanity. We have a tendency to look to authority figures to treat us well and take care of us, like a political 'nanny' who will look out for us and not let anyone hurt us. This is rather childish and wishful thinking, yet each generation hopes that the next political party who gets into office will do the right thing by them. But God's Word says that the heart of man is desperately wicked (see Jeremiah 17:9). The Book of Revelation shows us just how wicked and evil the totalitarian Antichrist regime will be. If we take a long hard look at what is happening in the world today, it would appear that this regime is now no longer a murky shadow on the side-lines. The Antichrist is arising in our lifetime, and all that is prophesied in the Bible will become more and more visible as the weeks and months unfold.

As Jesus has told us that, during the End Times, the love of many will grow cold, why do we cling to our hopes that this will not be the case? The forces of darkness are coming against the whole world and will remove from us the freedoms we have taken for granted in order to bring about a situation where individual nations will willingly hand over their sovereignty to a global leader. We will see this later in Chapter 6.

We are merely burying our heads in the sand if we reject the thought that secret plans of an elite, globalist agenda could be coming to the fore in our lifetime. If we investigate things that we read and hear about, and we find they are fake, then we can simply dismiss them. But if what is happening is true, and the global plans are part of the fulfilment of End Times prophecy, then we really are foolish if we continue to dismiss them as a conspiracy theory. Jesus has warned us to keep watch. He expects us to at least do a measure of research of world events in order to discern the signs of the times, and to see if the global agenda lines up with Bible prophecy. If it does, then woe be to us if we ignore it.

The Globalist Agenda

When the global elite have a plan, it will be heavily disguised as something good for all humanity, using a crisis to bring in their oppressive, totalitarian agenda. I read this extract from an article, dated 24th April 2020, on *Bleeding Edge Blog* which sums this up;

> "Today, the United Nations Chief warned of Authoritarian governments and tyrannical leaders weaponizing this Covid-19 pandemic in order to subvert Human Rights across the globe...
>
> At the United Nations, Secretary-General António Guterres warned Wednesday that authoritarian

governments are exploiting the pandemic to crack down on human rights. Indeed, Secretary-General António Guterres said this today: "Against the background of rising ethno-nationalism, populism, authoritarianism and the pushback against human rights in some countries, the crisis can provide a pretext to adopt repressive measures for purposes unrelated to the pandemic."

Note the last few lines in that quote.

To read the full article, visit the website https://beb. mobi/2020/04/24/the-welfare-of-humanity-is-always-the-alibi-of-tyrants/

It is well documented in the public domain that world governments desire an open, global society. Under the guise of 'transforming our world' through *The Sustainable Development Agenda*, the United Nations has created *Agenda 21*, which has now been upgraded to *Agenda 2030*, involving the world's central banks, governments, the media and science, all pushing for control of the world's population through some means.

Taken from the website www.thenewamerican.com, an extract from an article titled, "UN Agenda 2030: A Recipe for Global Socialism" dated January 6, 2016 reads,

"The United Nations and its mostly autocratic member regimes have big plans for your life, your children, your country, and your world…. Virtually every national government/dictatorship on the planet met at the 70th annual General Assembly at UN headquarters in New York in 2015 to adopt a draconian 15-year master plan for the planet…. Officially dubbed "Agenda 2030," the UN plot, as its full title suggests, is aimed at "transforming" the world. The program is a follow-up to the last 15-year UN plan, the defunct "Millennium Development Goals," or MDGs. It also dovetails nicely with the deeply controversial UN Agenda 21, even including much of the same rhetoric and agenda. But the combined Agenda 2030 goals for achieving what is euphemistically called "sustainable development" represent previous UN plans on steroids — deeper, more radical, more draconian, and more expensive."

(Link: https://www.thenewamerican.com/tech/environment/ item/22267-un-agenda-2030-a-recipe-for-global-socialism).

Add to this the plans of the billionaire philanthropist, George Soros' *Open Society Foundation*. Having been inspired by the philosophy of Karl Popper, Soros' idea is to usurp individual thought and belief with an overarching 'truth' that encompasses all of society.

The following information is from the website of www.philanthropydaily.com

"For Soros, one of the most important takeaways from Popper's ideas is that no single philosophy or worldview is in possession of the truth. Groups need to let go of "their truth" and work for an open society. But then it follows that the open society becomes, by default, the regnant paradigm, the overarching "truth" by which members of the society must live. If that's the case, there is ultimately no room for diversity of thought and ways of life. Acceptance of individualism and a casting off of traditional customs becomes a prerequisite for membership, because everything else is "totalitarian." Thus, what presents itself as the best type of society for embracing different ways of life is in reality the beginning of the greatest uniformity."

For more details, visit, https://www.philanthropydaily.com/ george-soros-karl-popper-and-the-ironies-of-the-open-society/

It is not my intention to discuss the above topics in any detail in this book as there is plenty of information online that you can research. Just bear in mind that any organization that has a sinister intent will pay substantial amounts to have their plans made appealing to the gullible, and they will pay equally handsome sums to quash whistle-blowers and any suggestion of a 'conspiracy theory'. They want the masses to believe that their plans are for the global good. And with this intent, they will spare no expense in achieving their goal.

Using the threat of 'Covid19 is not going away', with their vast financial resources, they employ the use of their 'bed-fellows' - the mainstream media – to heavily peddle the wearing of a facemask under the pretence that it will 'keep us safe'. At the same time, and for the same supposed reason, the media and world governments are ramping up the pressure concerning a global vaccination and ID programme. Using words like "We strongly encourage" or "We will use very strong campaigns", governments will use coercion, manipulation and even shame in their drive to get the public to accept the vaccine, using propaganda and the persuasive power of fear to cause people to crumble under the pressure to comply. The usual trick of 'it is better to be safe than sorry' will no doubt be the ploy that is hurled at those who refuse to have the vaccine.

Regarding the vaccine, the Australian Chief Medical Officer, Professor Paul Kelly, says,

"It will be the absolute ticket to get back to some sort of normal society and the things we all love."

(Link: https://www.theaustralian.com.au/news/latest-news/coronavirus-vaccine-should-be-mandatory-pm/news-story/fc7dc9cd495bcc7332487c07731b4c98).

Many Christians do not want to take the vaccine because of the potential of its future uses in global control. Yet, a coalition of more than 2,700 evangelical leaders is urging believers to have the vaccine. Using Jesus' Words that we are to 'love our neighbour as ourselves' (see Mark 12:31), on the website of an organization called *The BioLogos Foundation* these words can be found;

"Therefore, because of our faith in Jesus Christ, we will… wear masks…get vaccinated…mask rules are not experts taking away our freedom, but an opportunity to follow Jesus' command to love our neighbours as ourselves…" (Extracts from text on www.biologos.org)

A vaccine that has been rushed into production in a matter of months cannot pass as being safe. Some experts inform us that 10-15 years is required. Statistics have shown that the Covid19 virus is not the 'pandemic' threat that governments and the media have made it out to be. With the survival rate being 99.94%, this must surely indicate that we *do not* need a vaccine at all.

With the recovery figures being as high as they are, the continual insistence for a global vaccine containing our ID, medical and possibly financial details, and with an ability to track our every move, is a gross over-reaction. Such unrelenting measures indicate an intention that is beyond *simple* healthcare. It displays sinister intent disguised as something that will be for the *greater good* of humanity. People or organizations who are trying to deceive us are not going to outwardly say that they are deceiving us. They will pump millions into carefully-crafted advertising to give the outward appearance of doing us good, and inform us that what they are planning to do is going to be for our ultimate benefit. Nevertheless, the 'good' that they are promoting and doing could have totally evil intentions. These quotes come to mind:

'The welfare of humanity is always the alibi of tyrants.' — Albert Camus

'The urge to save humanity is almost always a false front for the urge to rule.' — H.L. Mencken

Many organizations cover up their evil plans by doing an abundance of 'good works' locally, nationally or globally, often giving away large donations to charities, so that they appear as generous and trustworthy people, with great integrity. But behind the scenes, all manner of evil may be going on. Many scandals of this nature have been exposed over the past 20 years, often leaving people numb with shock that certain celebrities, or other high-profile individuals, who they held in high regard, could ever use their positions of power and influence to perpetrate evil and abuse under the cloak of their charitable deeds.

Think of Satan's plan to deceive Adam and Eve in the Garden of Eden. He didn't go in there with his evil plan in full view! He deceived Eve with his *subtle* approach, telling her how good it would be for her and Adam if they accepted his advice on how to 'improve' their lives by gaining what they didn't currently have. This is how deceivers operate. They tell us that something is for our benefit, for our self-improvement and ultimately for the greater good of all humanity. Such claims really ought to make us 'smell a rat!'

Conditioning for the 'New Normal'

Those in power, who have plans to control the world, prime us gradually over a long period, to get us used to the idea of their plans, often using the media and entertainment industry as their platform. For example, over recent years, there have been several blockbuster movies with the theme of a global viral pandemic with the threat of global consequences, and a 'saviour' rising up to save humanity. At the time we most probably didn't think anything of it, but looking back with hindsight, do we not now scratch our heads and question whether these movies were priming us for a future real-life situation?

In a 2015 video, we find Bill Gates 'warning' of a global viral pandemic, using the coronavirus image as his example. This is quite astonishing considering this video was made 5 years *before* the outbreak of Covid19. Might he have 'known' something?

Additionally, in a 2015 *TED talk* video (https://www.youtube.com/watch?v=6Af6b_wyiwI), he refers to 'the next outbreak'.

In 2018, Bill and Melinda Gates stated that a global pandemic was on its way, adding that an engineered virus is humanity's greatest threat, and that this would happen in the next decade. Again, how could they possibly know this, let alone make such a definite statement?

(Link: https://australiannationalreview.com/state-of-affairs/ bill-and-melinda-gates-guaranteed-an-imminent-global-pandemic/)

Then in October 2019, just a matter of months before the Covid19 outbreak, a high-level global pandemic simulation called *Event 201* was undertaken by 15 global business, government and public health leaders. From the website www.centreforhealthsecurity.org under the heading 'Recommendations' it states;

> "The next severe pandemic will not only cause great illness and loss of life but could also trigger major cascading economic and societal consequences that could contribute greatly to global impact and suffering."

For more information, go to; https://www. centerforhealthsecurity.org/event201/recommendations.html

Let me repeat…this 'pandemic' simulation exercise was carried out just a couple of months *before* the Covid19 outbreak, which began in China in December 2019.

Since the outbreak, Gates has been heard to say,

> "We don't have a choice…for the world at large, normalcy only returns when we've largely vaccinated the entire global population."

(Link: https://www.youtube.com/watch?v=Art78dGqpQ4)

When we put all these things together; the pandemic themed movies, the 2015 video warning and the 2019 simulation exercise, the strange and unexplained circumstances surrounding the appearance of the virus, the wearing of face masks and the shaming and abuse dished out to those who are legitimately exempt from wearing one, the push for a global vaccine, the gradual reducing of the use of cash to create a cashless society, the promoting of digital ID technology for application onto the skin, the call to create a New World Order with a One World Religion; does all of this not make us question why world leaders would do this and what is really going on? Does this not make us see that we are gradually being 'conditioned' for the future; the global 'new normal' which is being described as *The Great Reset*? This is designed to be a global initiative where every nation must participate. Professor Klaus Schwab, Founder and Executive chairman of the *World Economic Forum* tells us rather chillingly that,

> "The pandemic represents a rare and narrow window of opportunity to reflect, reimagine and reset our world."

You can read this, and much more, on the *World Economic Forum* website, https://www.weforum.org/agenda/2020/06/now-is-the-time-for-a-great-reset/

We are living in unprecedented times, with rapid changes being made to our freedom and our way of life *without* our consent. We are being conditioned to toe-the-line and to comply with the collective narrative of what we are being programmed to accept as the new normal. Surely this warrants some level of investigation on our part, rather than tossed in the bin as a 'conspiracy theory'.

To conclude this long chapter, with all that we see happening in this world, wondering what unbelievable and unprecedented news we will wake up to each morning, in my own mind it is without question that all of this fits with End Times Bible prophecy. We are living in the birth pains era and are visibly approaching the time of the setting up of the New World Order with its appointing of the global leader. Whoever this person is, he will bring his 'solution' to the global chaos, and will bring about peace for 3½ years. At the end of that period the Church will then be raptured. This person will then be revealed as the Antichrist, and truly unimaginable hell will then break loose on this earth, upon those left behind to endure the wrath of God in the final 3½ years known as the Great Tribulation.

> "And there will be strange signs in the sun, moon, and stars. And here on earth the nations will be in turmoil, perplexed by the roaring seas and strange tides. **People will be terrified at what they see coming upon the earth,** for the powers in the heavens will be shaken."
> – Luke 21:25-26 NLT (Author's emphasis)

Having looked at the End Times birth pains and the Great Tribulation as given to us by Jesus in the New Testament, we will now look at both more fully.

In Chapter 5, we will be discussing **What will happen to the Church?** In our search for the whereabouts of the Bride of Christ we will be looking at Revelation chapters 4-6 to see what we can expect to be taking place upon the earth in the time of the birth pains.

Then in Chapter 6, we will look at the Great Tribulation, where we will work through Revelation chapters 8-22.

Chapter 5

WHAT WILL HAPPEN TO THE CHURCH? – THE RAPTURE OF BELIEVERS

"My beloved speaks and says to me,
'**Arise, my love,** my fair one,
And come away."
– Song of Solomon 2:10 AMP (Author's emphasis)

In the previous chapter, I touched on the subject of the Rapture of the Bride of Christ. As it is of such importance, it warrants a whole chapter of its own, and so I want to go into more detail to try to bring the subject into clearer light. It is a topic which causes much contention throughout the Church and has developed into three different camps; *pre-tribulation* (before the start of Revelation chapter 4), *mid-tribulation* (after the birth pains events which occur in Revelation chapters 4-6) and *post-tribulation* (at the end of the Great Tribulation). Interestingly, I have heard some Christians say they don't think there will be a Rapture of any kind at all.

Over the years many believers have felt tossed to-and-fro by the Church's confusion on this subject. I admit that I have got caught up in this confusion and didn't really know what to think. As it is the devil who brings confusion, I was adamant not to let him keep me in this befuddled state, so I decided to pray about the Rapture, and I asked the Lord to clarify it to me somehow. I had no idea how the Lord would do this, so I just left it with Him. A few days after I had prayed, He gave me a very vivid, powerful, all-encompassing dream of the Rapture in which my whole body was caught up in the experience. Every sinew of my being felt the intensity of being raised up from the earth and catapulted at the speed of light through the heavenly realms. It felt so physically real to me, I believed it had actually happened.

But then I woke up and found myself still in bed. I was overtaken by an immense feeling of fear because I thought the Rapture had happened and that I had been left behind! It took me a while to realise that the Rapture had not taken place and that the Lord had given me this dream in answer to my prayer and to reassure me of its reality. I can assure you that it has held me fast to the faithfulness of His Word, and to do all that I can to make sure I am ready for this event.

As is biblical, the Lord did *not give* me a date for the Rapture, but the scriptures are given to us to read and study, for in them we can find His guidance not only for every aspect of our life on earth, but also for what is to come. His Word is a lamp unto our feet and a light unto our path (see Psalm 119:105). Why do we think that God would only give us His light for our earthly existence but leave us in the dark in relation to our being taken out of this world and into His presence? His Word is the beacon shining in the darkness, lighting the way so that He can steer us away from the coming destruction and bring us safely into His kingdom.

Studying His Word will enable us to see at what point the Church's deliverance out of this world *may* occur, even though we will still not know when it will happen. This is why Jesus exhorts us to be watchful of the signs of the times and to make ourselves ready for His sudden return for His Bride.

Therefore, in view of the different schools of thought on this subject, let's see what God's Word has to say, because it is only from His Word that we will find the truth.

Whilst this first passage is written in relation to the Children of Israel, we can see that it would also apply to followers of Christ, as it mentions *"everyone who is found written in the Book of Life"*. If we are Christians, our names are written in the Lamb's Book of Life (see Revelation 3:5; 20:12; 21:27). Note in this passage it says we will be rescued. The word 'rescued' means being saved from a dangerous situation and taken to a place of safety.

> "Now at that [end] time Michael, the great [angelic] prince who stands guard over the children of your people, will arise. And there will be a time of distress such as never occurred since there was a nation until that time; but at that time your people, **everyone who is found written in the Book [of Life], will be rescued.** Many of those who sleep in the dust of the ground will awake (resurrect), these to everlasting life, but some to disgrace and everlasting contempt (abhorrence)." – Daniel 12:1-2 AMP (Author's emphasis)

Here are some scriptures from the New Testament:

> "But [we are different, because] our citizenship is in heaven. And from there we eagerly await [the coming of] the Savior, the Lord Jesus Christ; who, by exerting that power which enables Him even to subject everything to Himself, will [not only] transform [but completely refashion] our earthly bodies so that they will be like His glorious resurrected body." – Philippians 3:20-21 AMP

> "...and to [look forward and confidently] wait for [the coming of] His Son from heaven, whom He raised from the dead—**Jesus, who [personally] rescues us from the coming wrath [and draws us to Himself, granting us all the privileges and rewards of a new life with Him].**" – 1 Thessalonians 1:10 AMP (Author's emphasis)

> "For the Lord Himself will come down from heaven with a shout of command, with the voice of the archangel

and with the [blast of the] trumpet of God, and the dead in Christ will rise first. **Then we who are alive and remain [on the earth] will simultaneously be caught up (raptured) together with them [the resurrected ones] in the clouds to meet the Lord in the air, and so we will always be with the Lord!** Therefore comfort and encourage one another with these words [concerning our reunion with believers who have died]." – 1 Thessalonians 4:16-18 AMP (Author's emphasis)

"So then let us not sleep, as others do, but let us keep awake and be sober. For those who sleep, sleep at night, and those who get drunk, are drunk at night. But since we belong to the day, let us be sober, having put on the breastplate of faith and love, and for a helmet the hope of salvation. **For God has not destined us for wrath, but to obtain salvation through our Lord Jesus Christ,** who died for us so that whether we are awake or asleep we might live with him." – 1 Thessalonians 5: 6-10 ESV (Author's emphasis)

"And just as it is appointed for man to die once, and after that comes judgment, so Christ, having been offered once to bear the sins of many, will appear a second time, not to deal with sin **but to save those who are eagerly waiting for him.**" – Hebrews 9:27-28 ESV (Author's emphasis)

The parable of the Ten Virgins is a perfect example of the Rapture of the Bride of Christ. These are Jesus' own words, so we must surely believe His promise in this passage; a promise to take with Him those who are eagerly waiting for Him;

"Then the kingdom of heaven will be like ten virgins, who took their lamps and went to meet the bridegroom. Five of them were foolish [thoughtless, silly, and careless], and five were wise [far-sighted, practical, and sensible]. For when the foolish took their lamps, they did not take

any [extra] oil with them, but the wise took flasks of oil along with their lamps. Now while the bridegroom was delayed, they all began to nod off, and they fell asleep. But at midnight there was a shout, **'Look! The bridegroom [is coming]! Go out to meet him.'** Then all those virgins got up and put their own lamps in order [trimmed the wicks and added oil and lit them]. But the foolish virgins said to the wise, 'Give us some of your oil, because our lamps are going out.' But the wise replied, 'No, otherwise there will not be enough for us and for you, too; go instead to the dealers and buy oil for yourselves.' But while they were going away to buy oil, the bridegroom came, **and those who were ready went in with him to the wedding feast; and the door was shut and locked.** Later the others also came, and said, 'Lord, Lord, open [the door] for us.' But He replied, 'I assure you and most solemnly say to you, I do not know you [we have no relationship].' Therefore, be on the alert [be prepared and ready], for you do not know the day nor the hour [when the Son of Man will come]."
– Matthew 25:1-13 AMP (Author's emphasis)

The believers who will be taken with the Lord are represented in this parable as the five wise virgins. Wise believers are those who are faithful, repentant and obedient followers of Christ who are watching, waiting and ready for His return, when He will take them to be with Him. In this parable, Jesus says very clearly, *"Look! The bridegroom is coming! **Go out to meet him**"*. I find the words *"Go out to meet him"* immensely profound and prophetic. They imply that once we hear the shout that the Bridegroom is coming, those within the Church who fulfil the description of being wise believers will arise from wherever they are and *go out* of this world to *meet him* in the air at the Rapture.

The Jewish Wedding

The disciples would have fully understood Jesus' analogy of a

139

bridegroom coming for his bride. In the traditional Jewish wedding ceremony, after the groom had undertaken the betrothal, he would have left his bride for a period of at least twelve months and would return to his father's house to prepare a place for them both to live *in the father's house*. During this twelve-month separation, the bride would make herself ready for her beloved's return. She would begin to detach herself from her life as a single woman and focus solely on becoming the wife of the bridegroom, cleansing herself and making herself ready for his appearing.

When the marital accommodation was ready, the groom's father would be the one to decide the timing as to when his son could return to get his bride. She did not know when he would come, and neither did he; his father was the only one who would determine the time of his son's return, which would be like a thief in the night, when they least expected it. The bride and her maids had to be ready, at all times, for the sudden shout that the bridegroom was coming. They had to be ready to rise up and go out to meet the groom.

Jesus used this analogy for good reason; to instruct us that He is going to return for His Bride (those who are His followers) and remove her out of her earthly life and take her to be with Him within the Father's house. There is no other possible reason why Jesus used this analogy. The Rapture cannot be made any clearer.

For further information on the Jewish wedding, visit www.biblestudytools.com/commentaries/revelation/related-topics/the-jewish-wedding-analogy.html

Jesus also says,

> "Do not let your heart be troubled (afraid, cowardly). Believe [confidently] in God and trust in Him, [have faith, hold on to it, rely on it, keep going and] believe also in Me. In My Father's house are many dwelling places. If it were not so, I would have told you, because I am going there to prepare a place for you. And if I go and prepare a

place for you, **I will come back again and I will take you to Myself, so that where I am you may be also.**" – John 14:1-3 AMP (Author's emphasis)

The Word of God says that followers of Christ are *not* appointed to suffer God's wrath but to inherit salvation (see 1 Thessalonians 5:9), and to count themselves worthy to *escape all these things* that are coming upon the earth (see Luke 21:36). Therefore, it is clear that God has no intention of leaving the Bride of His Son (Jesus Christ) on this earth to go through what is only appointed to happen to those on the earth who have rejected Jesus as the Messiah and have rebelled against His Word. What sort of Bridegroom would Jesus be if He allowed His faithful Bride to experience the wrath of her heavenly Father, a wrath that is reserved solely for unbelievers and the wilfully unrepentant?

God's wrath upon the *unbelieving* world will be poured out after the revealing of the Antichrist which will begin the final 3½ years of the Great Tribulation. This commences in Revelation 8, which we will study in Chapter 6.

The Lord will remove His watching and waiting Bride from the earth before the horrors of the Great Tribulation unfold.

The Rapture of the Church (the Bride of Christ) in the Book of Revelation

I want to set out, in chronological order, the sequence of events shown in the Book of Revelation chapters 4 to 6, so that we can see clearly what is to happen. Jesus is *not* the author of confusion. He did not appoint His angel to give the Apostle John a haphazard vision of the things to come and then leave him to work out for himself in what order the events would occur! No, on the contrary, Jesus' Word tells us the order of events, and it is up to us to believe it.

Before we look at Revelation chapters 4-6, I want to mention that in chapters 1-3 of the Book of Revelation, Jesus gives His End Times letters to the churches, encouraging them in the things that they are doing well, but rebuking and warning them about the things that they are doing which are not in keeping with His Word. He warns them to repent of these things. If they fail to heed His warnings, they will face great consequences. I wrote about this in my book, *Come on Church! Wake Up!* You can find details of this at the end of this book.

Jesus' warnings in Revelation chapters 1-3 apply to us today, the 21st century Church throughout the whole world. It would serve us well if we took time out to read these, so that as individuals, we can examine our own lives and do whatever is necessary to get ourselves ready for Jesus' return.

But firstly, before the full unveiling of the End Times vision was given to the Apostle John by the angel of the Lord, Jesus actually promised us something;

> "Because you have kept the word of My endurance [My command to persevere], **I will keep you [safe] from the hour of trial,** that hour which is about to come on the whole [inhabited] world, to test those who live on the earth." – Revelation 3:10 AMP (Author's emphasis)

In this verse, Jesus has made a promise to His followers to keep them safe *from* the hour of trial that is coming upon the earth.

In relation to this verse, in his book, *The Last Hour – An Israeli Insider Looks at the End Times,* author Amir Tsarfati says,

> 'The word translated "from" is the Greek word *ek*, which means "out of." This means that the Church will be kept out of the hour of tribulation, not *through*.' [1]

Let's allow this to really sink into the depths of our being so that we will believe it.

Jesus did not say He would keep us safe *in* the hour of trial; He said, *from* the hour of trial. We need to grasp this truth. If He was going to keep us safe in the trial, that means we would remain in the Great Tribulation. But as He has clearly stated that He will keep us safe *from* (out of) the trial, it must surely be without doubt that Jesus is going to keep us safe from the trial by *removing* us from it, in the same way that a fireman would remove us from a burning building to keep us safe from its destruction.

Tsarfati concurs;

'The Church is not slated for the Tribulation punishment. Paul praises the Thessalonians for their commitment "to wait for His Son from heaven, whom He raised from the dead, even Jesus who delivers us from the wrath to come." (1 Thessalonians 1:10).

Wrath is not for the people of God.' [2]

It is so easy for us to gloss over Jesus' promise of deliverance, and not really take on board what it means. The words of Revelation 3:10 are powerful words from our Saviour, literally promising to *save us* from the wrath of God that is coming. Why do we not see this? Why do so many believers debate, dispute and even reject what Jesus has clearly said?

In light of the above, although the Church is not specifically mentioned after Revelation chapter 3 - causing many to believe that the Church is raptured at that point (before the birth pains period written about in Revelation chapters 4-6) - if we study the scriptures deeper, we will discover something that has taken me 28 years to realise: I agree that there is no mention of the Church after the end of Revelation chapter 3, but does that imply that the Church is no longer on the earth?

Before you throw your hands up and toss this book into the bin because of the comment I have just made, I humbly ask if you would kindly bear with me so that we can look at this in a bit more depth. After the end of Revelation 3, the next time the scriptures mention the body of believers is in Revelation 7:9-17, where the angel gives John a vision of the great multitude from every nation, robed in white, standing before the throne of God. However, between the end of Revelation 3 and the appearance of the great multitude in white in Revelation 7, a whole host of global events occur, which are graphically described in Revelation chapters 4-6. As I have mentioned, I believe this is the period of the time of the birth pains, the events of which are described in the first five seals in Revelation chapter 6, which we will look at shortly. The end of Revelation 6 (verses 12-17) culminates with the opening of the sixth seal, which is the commencement of the outpouring of the wrath of God on the rebellious and unbelieving world.

If the beginnings of the birth pains events (the beginning of sorrows) began in 1948, (when Israel became a nation again and her people began to return to the land God covenanted to them), it is possible that the final period of the birth pains (the events of the first five seals preceding the Great Tribulation) could be the initial 3½ years of the actual 7 year Tribulation period.

The events of the time of the birth pains will precede the *revealing* of the Antichrist, although he is highly likely to be on the earth in his human form being prepared for his role as global leader to bring in his deceptive 7-year peace treaty which the world will believe will bring global peace, safety and security. After he has been in office as the global leader for 3½ years, his metamorphosis into the embodiment of the Antichrist will begin the final 3½ year period of the Great Tribulation, which will be the outpouring of the wrath of God on all unbelievers and those left behind who claimed to be Christians but were not living their lives in readiness for His appearing. The Church will certainly no longer be on the earth when that event occurs. But if believers are not raptured *prior* to the time of the birth pains, (i.e. at the end of Revelation chapter 3) then the Church would still be on the earth *during* the time of the birth pains. We will look at this further ahead under the sub-heading '**The Question of the Rapture**'.

So, let's now take this opportunity to look at the End Times visions that the angel of the Lord showed the Apostle John relating to the times of the birth pains (the possible initial 3½ years of the Tribulation).

Below I have given a summary, but I ask that you would not rely solely on my text; I strongly encourage you to read the chapters in your own Bible. In some of the summaries I have commented on the text.

Revelation 4: A Vision of Heaven

Summary – Verses 1-11

> John sees a door open in heaven and he is told that he must be shown what will soon take place. He then sees the throne of God in all its glory and the One who sits on it. He also sees the twenty-four elders who are dressed in white with gold crowns on their heads. They are sitting on thrones around the throne of God. He sees and hears lightning, rumblings, and thunder coming from the throne of God. There are four creatures around the throne; they are covered with eyes and have six wings and they praise the Lord day and night. As they do so, the twenty-four elders fall down to worship and praise the Lord and lay their crowns before the throne.

Revelation 5: The Lamb and the Scroll

This begins the opening of the seven seals.

My comments: When an important document is bound with a wax seal, the importance of the contents of the document that is sealed remains hidden until a specific, appointed time. At that appointed time when the seal is opened, the contents of the document are made known to all to whom the sealed document pertains. The seal is opened, the contents are revealed, and they cannot be reversed.

Once the first seal of the Book of Revelation has been opened, from that moment on, the world is on the *final* countdown towards Jesus' Second Coming. As the events of a seal are fulfilled upon the earth, each successive seal is opened in turn and the whole world will experience the consequences that each seal reveals. Let's discover what is going to occur as the Lamb (Jesus) opens the seals on the scroll.

Summary – Verses 1-14

John then sees a scroll in God's right hand, sealed with seven seals. A mighty angel speaks loudly, asking, *"Who is worthy to break the seals and open the scroll?"* (Verse 2 NIV). No one in heaven, on the earth, or under the earth could open it, and John weeps. But then he is told that the Lion of Judah has triumphed and is able to open the scroll. A Lamb appears, standing in the centre of the throne and it looks as if it has been slain. The Lamb takes the scroll and the twenty-four elders fall down before the Lamb. The elders hold golden bowls full of incense, which are the prayers of the saints (all the prayers of every true believer). The elders worship the Lamb, saying that He is worthy to open the seals of the scroll because He was slain and shed His blood to redeem people for God from every tribe, language, and nation. Then John sees and hears the voice of thousands upon thousands of angels around the throne, worshiping the Lamb that was slain. Then every creature in heaven, on the earth, under the earth, on the sea, and in the sea joins in singing worship to the Lamb. The four creatures around the throne say "Amen" and the elders fall down in worship. The Lamb is Jesus.

Revelation 6: The Opening of the First Six Seals

The following is what we will begin to experience upon the earth once Jesus has opened the first seal. After that, all successive seals are opened. These are the things we need to be awake and alert to and not casually dismiss.

Summary – Verses 1-2: The first seal

John sees the Lamb open the first seal, and a rider appears on a white horse wearing a crown and carrying a bow in his hand. He rides out as a conqueror determined on conquest. Because this rider is on a white horse and wears a crown, many think this rider is Jesus. But this cannot be the case because the events this rider brings take place *prior* to the time when Jesus returns at His Second Coming, which is recorded in Revelation 19:11–16, which we will look at later.

My comments: I believe the rider mentioned in this first seal represents an earthly kingdom (or perhaps several nations joined together as a global alliance), as indicated by the crown. This kingdom or alliance is bent on 'riding' across the world in a defiant manner conquering other kingdoms and nations. The bow indicates a kingdom that is determined on using force to bring about submission, and will not stop until it has succeeded in its conquering.

This describes what we are experiencing in our current time. Kingdoms exist and others are rising up at this very time, bent on destruction, steadily pushing their way into territories and nations, overthrowing them, and establishing their own rule over these lands, including imposing their own laws in place of the existing laws of the nations they intend to conquer, to bring about global submission. The spirit of the Antichrist has been in the world since the time of Christ, but it would seem that the opening of this first seal releases the End Times spirit of the Antichrist which will escalate upon the earth, as we will see.

Summary – Verses 3-4: The second seal

John sees the Lamb open the second seal and a rider on a fiery red horse appears. This rider is given a large sword, and he is given power to take peace from the earth, and causes people to kill each other.

My comments: This would indicate a time where the peace we have taken for granted is suddenly removed, not just nationally but globally. There will be global unrest, fear and distress, insecurity, and uncertainty. One moment peace is agreed, and the next moment it is destroyed, resulting in people killing each other through protests and riots, civil war and nations warring against other nations for whatever reason. Jesus warned us of these times in the Gospels. The large sword could represent the large-scale killing that will occur.

This very scenario has been happening around the world throughout the decades, but it is now escalating in 2020.

Summary – Verses 5-6: The third seal

John sees the Lamb open the third seal, and he sees another rider, this time on a black horse. The rider holds a pair of scales in his hand and John hears a voice saying there would be a quart of wheat for a day's wages and three quarts of barley for a day's wages and not to damage the oil and the wine.

My comments: As a result of the distress of the first two seals, the world will become increasingly unstable due to unrelenting war and broken peace treaties, resulting in global economies collapsing and causing prices to rise so high that it will cost people a day's wages for a loaf of bread—not just in a few under-developed countries but globally, including all the superpower nations. In the Gospels, Jesus warns us about these famines.

When we look at the world today, we can see the evidence of this right across the globe, and this situation is on the increase.

Summary – Verses 7-8: The fourth seal

John sees the Lamb open the fourth seal. This time he sees a pale horse with another rider. The rider's name is Death. Hades (hell) follows close behind him. *They* (that is Hades and the rider called Death) are given power over a quarter of the earth to kill with the sword, with famine, with the plague, and by wild beasts.

My comments: As a result of the catastrophes of the first three seals, people will die from starvation, plagues, and being attacked and killed by wild animals, probably because the animals are also starving due to worldwide famines. 'Killing by the sword' could mean that people are killing each other because they are fighting over what little food there is available, as well as being killed by the sword in conflict, persecution and terrorism. In the passage, it mentions that Hades (hell) follows close behind all of this death. This could indicate that many who die during the period of this devastating fourth seal will end up in hell.

All of the things in this passage are happening on the earth right now.

Summary – Verses 9-11: The fifth seal

John sees the Lamb open the fifth seal, and he sees under the altar the souls of all those who have been martyred because of the Word of God and the testimony they have maintained. These souls cry out in a loud voice asking the Lord how much longer it will be before He brings judgement upon the world in order to avenge their blood that has been shed for maintaining their faith even unto death. John sees each of them being given a white robe, and they are told to wait a little longer until the number of fellow servants who are yet to be martyred is completed.

My comments: This would indicate a time following all the global events of the previous four seals, where many who say they are a follower of Jesus Christ will be killed for their faith. The slaughter of Christians has been happening for centuries in countries that are opposed to the Christian faith. But this persecution is now spreading to countries that have been *established* on Christian foundations, such as the United Kingdom and the United States of America. Followers of Christ are now being hounded to death all across the world simply for believing in Him.

Before we look at what will happen when the Lamb opens the sixth seal, let's summarise, in order, the events of the first five seals.

1. A kingdom (or a global alliance of nations) will ride roughshod over the nations of the earth, bent on overthrowing and conquering every nation in its path, to bring about global submission.

2. This will bring about the end of peace, and this conquering kingdom will cause people to kill each other.

3. This will lead to global unrest, instability, and economic collapse so that prices rise, resulting in famines and starvation because people can't afford to buy food.

4. This in turn will bring about death through starvation, the outbreak of plagues, and people being killed by the sword and by wild beasts across a quarter of the world.

5. Many who try to speak about Jesus will be killed.

Since hearing the words 'The Unveiling of Revelation' for the year 2010, I have been stunned into a silence of reverential fear and trembling at what I have been witnessing just on our mainstream news. First it was some sort of 'Breaking News' perhaps once a week, but then increased to a few times each week. But now, in 2020, we are in a time where dramatic Breaking News is covered from morning to night, with more and more uploaded onto the TV screen, interrupting the main Breaking News with further Breaking News. Almost everything that is reported seems to be overwhelming, catastrophic and devastating.

Reading all of the above, one would think that the first five seals were already open! Has it ever occurred to us that perhaps they are? Let me explain: The opening of the seven seals is something that happens in the heavenly realms, and then the events contained in each seal begin to manifest on the earth. However, because of the complacency and indifference many Christians have concerning the Book of Revelation, it is possible that they might think they are actually going to visibly see the Four Horsemen of the Apocalypse galloping across the sky! But because they haven't seen any sign of them yet, they reject the possibility that the seals might already be open. I realise that some people may think I am deluded in what I have just said, but my response to this is that the seals have to be opened at some point in time, so why do we think that they are still sealed up when the evidence of what is written in these seals appears to be converging on this planet all at the same time? Courage is needed when we want to understand something that baffles us. Jesus has told us to keep watch for the signs of the times in order to know when 'His return is very near, right at the door' (see Matthew 24:33). We open ourselves up to delusion when we are not keeping watch as Jesus commanded. This delusion comes from Satan who wants as many believers as possible to be *unwatchful* and *unready* for Jesus' return.

As I mentioned earlier in this book, the words the Lord gave me in sequence were:

- 2010 – The Unveiling of Revelation
- 2011 – Death and Destruction
- 2012 – Cataclysmic Collapse
- 2013 – Escalation
- 2014-2019 – Continuance of the escalation

I have kept watch and seen that these words are being fulfilled. We must remind ourselves that once the first seal is open, it *cannot be reversed*, and all the events of all the subsequent seals will follow, as prophesied. They will continue on an escalating basis until the end comes. I believe that the first five seals have been opened and the world is experiencing these birth pain events more and more, and all that remains is for the Church to be raptured, and the 144,000 servants of the Lord to be sealed (which we are going to study after we have looked at the events of the sixth seal). Once these two events occur, the Lamb can open the sixth seal which will begin God's wrath upon the earth. However, I fully accept that many may hold a differing view. Whether the first five seals are already open or not, let's have a look at what the sixth seal holds in store for the world.

Summary – Verses 12-17: The sixth seal

> John sees the Lamb open the sixth seal. There is a great earthquake and the sun turns black, the moon turns blood red, and the stars fall to the earth. The sky is rolled up like a scroll and every mountain and island is removed from its place. Every king, prince, and general, along with the rich, the mighty, and every slave and free person hides themselves in caves and among the rocks. They all cry out for the mountains and rocks to fall on them, to hide them *"from the face of the one who sits on the throne and from the wrath of the Lamb"* (verse 16) because this is the great day of the wrath of God and the Lamb upon the face of the earth.

My comments: I think we would all agree that this event has not yet occurred upon the earth. It would seem that at a certain point during the events of the fifth seal (believers who have been martyred for their faith), God's patience over the sin and evil in this world will come to an end and He will bring about these cataclysmic events of the sixth seal upon the world. When this day of the wrath of God occurs, it will cause everyone left on the earth - from the least to the greatest - to flee for their lives. They will be desperate to be buried under rocks and in caves in order to hide from the wrath of God and the Lamb because of their rebellion and refusal to repent of their sins.

If this begins the time of the wrath of God upon the *unbelieving and rebellious people* of this world, where is the Church?

The Question of the Rapture

Many believers question at what point the Church will be raptured. As I said earlier, no mention of this long-awaited event is made anywhere in the text of Revelation chapters 4-6; nor did the angel of the Lord show John the Rapture at the end of Revelation chapter 3. For 28 years this has puzzled me.

I have personally believed, and still want to believe, in a pre-tribulation Rapture, which is that the Church will not have to go through the experience of the events of the birth pains (the first five seals). However, this belief seems to be contrary to scripture because in the Gospels, Jesus warns believers about the birth pains events, and says that we will see these things begin to happen. For too long, I have ignored what has been right in front of my eyes when I have read Jesus' words concerning the End Times.

Here is a question: How can believers see these things happen if we have already been raptured before they begin and are no longer on the earth to witness them?

Knowing all the different thoughts that people have on this subject, which has led to the rise of the three views about the timing of the Rapture; pre-tribulation, mid-tribulation and post-tribulation, I have found myself having to look really deeply at what is written in the Book of Revelation, and the order in which the events are all *revealed* to John. Having taken a lot of time to do this, I would like to share this with you.

What did I Discover?

As I mentioned earlier, Jesus instructed His angel to tell the Apostle John to send His letters to the churches, encouraging them in the good they were doing, and rebuking, correcting and exhorting them to repent of the sins which they were allowing, condoning and even practicing in their churches. He warned them that consequences would come if they failed to heed His warnings.

He also warned them of the things to come, and promised rewards to those who overcome. Revelation chapters 1 to 3 contain these vital messages to the Church.

Here is another question: Why would Jesus write these letters to believers if, at the close of His letters (at the completion of Revelation 3), He was then going to immediately Rapture the Church up to heaven before the period of the birth pains which He warned believers to be watchful for in the Gospels (i.e. a pre-tribulation Rapture)? This just doesn't make sense.

The fact that the Church is not specifically mentioned after Revelation 3 does not definitively mean that it has been raptured at *that* point. It would seem more likely that Jesus sent His warning letters to the churches to get themselves right, knowing that they would have to endure the period of the birth pains which unfolds through Revelation chapter 5 and fully unravels in Revelation chapter 6, culminating at the end of Revelation 6:11 (the completion of the fifth seal). Let's remind ourselves again that in Matthew chapter 24, Jesus actually warns believers to keep watch for the signs of the birth pains, and that we will experience these events! I repeat, why would Jesus warn us of this nearly 2,000 years ago, if it was His intention to Rapture us before they even began? How could we look for these signs of the times if we are not here on the earth to witness them?!

As much as I have found it hard to discover this, it appears to me that a pre-tribulation Rapture (before the beginning of any of the birth pains events) doesn't seem to fit with what Jesus has said in Matthew chapter 24, together with the purpose of His warning letters to the churches in Revelation chapters 1-3.

So, if believers are not taken up into heaven *before* the opening of the first seal, we would have to conclude that the Church is still on the earth to witness the time of the birth pains described in the first five seals of Revelation chapters 6, which we have just read.

If the Church is on the earth during this time, based on Jesus' promise in Revelation 3:10, we must believe that Jesus will deliver us out of this world before the final period of the great wrath of God falls upon the earth; the Great Tribulation which commences with the opening of the sixth seal in Revelation 6:12-17 (which we have looked at). The Church being taken out of the earth immediately before the Great Tribulation is known as the mid-tribulation Rapture. We will have a look at this shortly, to see if it fits in with what is written in the Book of Revelation.

But before that, let's see what else the Apostle John is shown at the start of the great wrath of the sixth seal. In Revelation chapter 7 it seems as if the angel of the Lord shows John a 'pause', a specific interlude revealing something that happens *at the same time as* the commencement of the unleashing of God's wrath on the earth at the end of Revelation chapter 6.

The Interlude

I recently read on social media that someone, who professed to be a Christian, believed, and was teaching people, that the vision of Revelation chapter 7 given to the Apostle John was a 'parenthesis'; supposedly an additional statement that was *stuck in* to the Book of Revelation, with *no time element attached to it*. I found this to be a most bizarre thing to believe, let alone teach it to believers.

As Jesus is not the author of confusion, it would surely be contrary to His nature to instruct His angel to randomly stick something in the middle of a whole host of chronological visions, knowing that to do so would leave believers in confusion about the order of End Times events. The events of the vision of Revelation chapter 7 are written directly *after* what the Apostle John wrote concerning the vision recorded in Revelation chapters 4-6. What is shown to John in Revelation 7 *has* to be fulfilled *before* the unstoppable outpouring of the wrath of God shown from Revelation chapter 8 onwards (which we will see later in Chapter 6).

So, let's have a look at this vision given in Revelation 7. It seems there is a momentary interlude where God's angels are told to hold back from unleashing further destruction upon the earth.

The first part of the interlude

John is firstly shown that four angels are commanded to seal the foreheads of the 144,000 servants of the Lord from the twelve tribes of Israel:

Revelation 7:2-8 ESV

This is the biblical text.

> "Then I saw another angel ascending from the rising of the sun, with the seal of the living God, and he called with a loud voice to the four angels who had been given power to harm earth and sea, saying, "Do not harm the earth or the sea or the trees, until we have sealed the servants of our God on their foreheads." And I heard the number of the sealed, 144,000, sealed from every tribe of the sons of Israel:
>
> 12,000 from the tribe of Judah were sealed,
> 12,000 from the tribe of Reuben,
> 12,000 from the tribe of Gad,
> 12,000 from the tribe of Asher,
> 12,000 from the tribe of Naphtali,
> 12,000 from the tribe of Manasseh,
> 12,000 from the tribe of Simeon,
> 12,000 from the tribe of Levi,
> 12,000 from the tribe of Issachar,
> 12,000 from the tribe of Zebulun,
> 12,000 from the tribe of Joseph,
> 12,000 from the tribe of Benjamin were sealed."

Concerning the seal on these people's heads, the Amplified Bible footnote says, 'The seal indicates both ownership and protection by God'.

These 144,000 men are specially chosen and sealed because, further on in Revelation 14:4-5 (AMP) it says;

"These are the ones who have not been defiled [by relations] with women, for they are celibate. These are the ones who follow the Lamb wherever He goes. These have been purchased and redeemed from among men [of Israel] as the first fruits [sanctified and set apart for special service] for God and the Lamb. No lie was found in their mouth, for they are blameless (spotless, untainted, beyond reproach)."

There are many views about the number of these people, whether literal or symbolic, but regardless of the actual number, most believers agree that, during the Great Tribulation, the purpose of these 'sealed' servants of the Lord will be to witness to the world, and in particular to the unbelieving Jews who still have not accepted Jesus as their Messiah, to bring them to faith in Him before His Second Coming.

The second part of the interlude

After the angel of the Lord has shown the Apostle John the birth pains events mentioned in Revelation chapter 6, and the sealing of God's protection being placed on the foreheads of the special 144,000 Jewish followers of Jesus Christ (Messianic Jews), John is then shown the mind-blowing vision of the multitude of the faithful in heaven!

Taking into account the fact that God is not the author of confusion and that He would not present to us the events of the End Times in a haphazard order, it is at this point in the Book of Revelation that I believe the angel of the Lord is showing John that the Bride of Christ has been raptured and is standing before the throne of God. We are going to look at this passage of scripture very shortly.

I believe that the Rapture occurs in the twinkling of an eye, at the precise moment that the sixth seal of God's wrath is opened, which also occurs at the same time as the sealing of those special 144,000 Jewish followers of Christ who will go out to preach the Gospel during the Great Tribulation period, especially to their own people, the nation of Israel. I believe that all three events occur simultaneously, but because each event is written in our Bibles separately, (with chapters and verses inserted by editors in the 15th and 16th century) our finite understanding seems to make the assumption that each event happens separately and is not related to the others. Yes, the angel of the Lord shows John each event as a sequence of separate visions, but if we remove the chapter numbers, headings and verse numbers (none of which appeared in the original scriptures), these visions all unfold one into the other as a panoramic story of the future. But let's remind ourselves that it was Jesus Himself who instructed John to write down the visions;

"Write down what you have seen—both the things that are now happening and the things that will happen."
– Revelation 1:19 NLT

Because they are written down as an account of separate visions, we can be left to think that the opening of the sixth seal, the sealing of the 144,000 and the vision of the great multitude in heaven are all separate events one after the other, when in fact it is very possible that all three occur at the same time. But in the written form, it may seem difficult to convey this to our natural understanding.

So, it is my conclusion that for faithful believers (both Jewish and Gentile believers) who have made themselves ready for the return of the Bridegroom (see the parable of the Ten Virgins), Jesus comes to snatch them out of the world after the completion of the birth pains of the first five seals in Revelation 6:1-11 (mid-tribulation), before God begins to unleash His final Great Tribulation wrath on the rest of humanity who are left on the earth (the world of unbelievers and those who professed faith in Christ but who refused to repent of their sins or obey His Word).

In Thayer's Greek Lexicon, the word for this 'snatching away' event is *harpazō*. Its meaning is;

- to seize, carry off by force.
- to seize on, claim for one's self eagerly.
- to snatch out or away.

Additionally, the Latin word for harpazo is *rapturo* from where we derive the English word Rapture.

This describes the coming of Jesus, the Bridegroom, to seize, carry off by force, snatch away and claim for Himself His Bride (His faithful followers) from the earth just moments before the final wrath of God is poured out upon the world. Once His Bride is safely in His Father's house, the angels will then be commanded to release the destruction that is in store for those left on the earth during the time of the Great Tribulation, which commences in Revelation chapter 8.

Let's now look at this beautiful passage of scripture concerning the vision of the raptured Bride of Christ standing before the throne of God; the event that every Christian should be yearning for and making themselves ready for.

Revelation 7:9-17 KJ21

"After this I beheld, and lo, a great multitude, which no man could number, of all nations and kindreds and people and tongues, stood before the throne and before the Lamb, clothed in white robes and with palms in their hands.

And they cried with a loud voice, saying, "Salvation to our God who sitteth upon the throne, and unto the Lamb!"

And all the angels stood round about the throne, and about the elders and the four living beings, and fell on their faces before the throne and worshiped God, saying,

"Amen. Blessing and glory and wisdom and thanksgiving, and honor and power and might, be unto our God for ever and ever. Amen!"

And one of the elders answered, saying unto me, "Who are these that are arrayed in white robes, and from whence have they come?"

And I said unto him, "Sir, thou knowest." And he said to me, "These are they that came out of great tribulation, and have washed their robes and made them white in the blood of the Lamb.

Therefore, "they are before the throne of God, and serve Him day and night in His temple; and He that sitteth on the throne shall dwell among them.

They shall hunger no more, neither thirst any more; neither shall the sun light on them, nor any heat.

For the Lamb who is in the midst of the throne shall feed them, and shall lead them unto living fountains of waters, and God shall wipe away all tears from their eyes."

The angel of the Lord has shown John the great multitude in white robes, from every nation of the world, standing before the throne of God and the Lamb. He is told that these people are those who have 'come out of great tribulation'. It does not say they have come out of *the* great tribulation, although many modern translations of the Bible have changed this text to read 'the great tribulation', which effectively changes its whole meaning. This text is saying that the multitude in white have been delivered from great tribulation (which I believe we can take to mean every type of persecution), which includes tribulation that has occurred at any time since Christ ascended into heaven. These words 'come out of' are the same as the words of the promise that Jesus made to the churches in Revelation 3:10, and also concur with the description of the word *harpazō*, meaning to 'snatch away'. To 'come out of great tribulation' would suggest that believers must be *in* a period of great tribulation *to some degree,* such as being on the earth during the earlier part, i.e., the time of the birth pains. Surely we can see that the birth pain events are a time of 'great tribulation' in themselves, although they are not the events of the wrath of God that will occur in the final 3½ years of the Great Tribulation. This is why I believe the Church will be raptured at the end of the birth pains, which I have suggested before, is mid-tribulation.

As the angel of the Lord has shown John the raptured believers in heaven at this *specific* point in the chronological order of the vision, and not previously such as at the end of Revelation chapter 3 (which would be pre-tribulation), surely this would indicate where the Rapture occurs in the sequence of the End Times events.

If this is truly the case, once the Church has been taken from the earth, the opening of the seventh seal (in Revelation chapter 8) begins the full onslaught of the Great Tribulation wrath of God on the world of unbelievers, and also Christians who have been left behind because they were not ready for His appearing; living complacent lives 'in the world'. To love the things of this world more than loving God means that we are at enmity with God (see James 4:4). We can't expect to be taken up in the Rapture to be with the Lord forever if we love the things of this world more than Him.

We will look fully at the Great Tribulation period in the next chapter.

For now, I would like to briefly show you two other places in the Book of Revelation where specific groups of believers are taken up into heaven at different times, to be with the Lord. I have never heard this mentioned in any church services that I have attended in the 28 years that I have been a follower of Christ, but it is something that is written in scripture, and as such, is worthy of mention.

Firstly, I would bring to your attention;

Revelation 11:7-12

In Revelation 11:3-6, John is shown the appearance of God's two End Times witnesses whose purpose it is to prophesy for 3½ years during the Great Tribulation. This occurs after the rapture of the Church. One can assume that their prophesying will be regarding judgement and salvation, exhorting those left on the earth to repent and believe in Christ before He returns at His Second Coming to judge the world.

Let's now read the passage, from verses 7-12, to see what happens to these two witnesses *after* they have finished the work that the Lord has given them to do;

> "Now when they have finished their testimony, the beast that comes up from the Abyss will attack them, and overpower and kill them. Their bodies will lie in the public square of the great city—which is figuratively called Sodom and Egypt—where also their Lord was crucified. For 3½ days some from every people, tribe, language and nation will gaze on their bodies and refuse them burial. The inhabitants of the earth will gloat over them and will celebrate by sending each other gifts, because these two prophets had tormented those who live on the earth.
>
> But after the 3½ days the breath of life from God entered them, and they stood on their feet, and terror struck those who saw them. **Then they heard a loud voice from heaven saying to them, "Come up here." And they went up to heaven in a cloud, while their enemies looked on.**" – Revelation 11:7-12 NIV (Author's emphasis)

As we can see, these two witnesses will experience their own personal Rapture into heaven.

Next, I bring to your attention the Rapture of the 144,000 servants of the Lord from the twelve tribes of Israel;

Revelation 14:2-3

After these specially chosen and sealed men have completed their task of preaching the Gospel during the Great Tribulation, we then see, in the following passage, that they too have arrived in heaven *before* the final Second Coming of Christ when He returns to set up His millennial reign. They have been *redeemed* from the earth, whilst it is still in existence. Redemption means to be delivered from something bad, such as sin, but it also refers to being delivered out of a bad situation; in this sense being redeemed *from* the Tribulation on the earth.

In the King James Dictionary (https://av1611.com/kjbp/kjv-dictionary/redeem.html) part of the definition of the word *redeem* says,

'To rescue; to recover; to deliver from.'

So, in this passage of scripture we see that the 144,000 will have a personal Rapture.

"And I heard a sound from heaven like the roar of rushing waters and like a loud peal of thunder. The sound I heard was like that of harpists playing their harps. And they sang a new song before the throne and before the four living creatures and the elders. No one could learn the song except **the 144,000 who had been redeemed from the earth.**" – Revelation 14:2-3 NIV (Author's emphasis)

This concludes our look at the Rapture of faithful and obedient believers.

But what about those who profess to be Jesus' followers, yet whom He considers to be amongst those whom He will *not* take with Him; those who are living their lives to please themselves and have not made themselves ready for His appearing? As Jesus is clearly going to leave them behind on the earth to endure the Great Tribulation (commencing in Revelation chapter 8), will the immense time of trial cause them to repent? Will they be saved? Let's have a look.

Believers who are Left Behind

As we saw earlier, the parable of the Ten Virgins not only shows us the Rapture of faithful and ready believers, it also shows us what will happen to believers who are *not ready* when Jesus returns for His Bride. I would encourage you to read it again to remind yourself of it (Matthew 25:1-13) before moving on to the scriptures that follow.

At the future time of the events mentioned in the passage below, the wrath of God will be well under way, with unspeakable, unrelenting anguish and pain being brought to bear upon those who are left behind. This is God's rightful justice upon all who rejected His son Jesus Christ, and all who professed allegiance to Him yet lived their lives more like that of the devil.

Let's read this and allow the severity of the situation to impact us deeply. This is the Word of the Lord.

> "So the four angels, who had been prepared for the hour, the day, the month, and the year, were released to kill a third of mankind. The number of mounted troops was twice ten thousand times ten thousand; I heard their number. And this is how I saw the horses in my vision and those who rode them: they wore breastplates the color of fire and of sapphire and of sulfur, and the heads of the horses were like lions' heads, and fire and smoke and sulfur came out of their mouths. By these three plagues a third of mankind was killed, by the fire and smoke and sulfur coming out of their mouths. For the power of the horses is in their mouths and in their tails, for their tails are like serpents with heads, and by means of them they wound. The rest of mankind, who were not killed by these plagues, **did not repent** of the works of their hands nor give up worshiping demons and idols of gold and silver and bronze and stone and wood, which cannot see or hear or walk nor did they repent of their murders or their

sorceries or their sexual immorality or their thefts."
– Revelation 9:15-21 ESV (Author's emphasis)

Further ahead in the Book of Revelation, in chapter 16, the seven angels of the Lord are pouring out the seven bowls of God's wrath, but astonishingly, despite the most horrendous suffering, justly coming to them by the hand of God, the people left behind on the earth will still refuse to repent.

> "The fourth angel poured out his bowl on the sun, and it was allowed to scorch people with fire. They were scorched by the fierce heat, and they cursed the name of God who had power over these plagues. **They did not repent and give him glory.**
>
> The fifth angel poured out his bowl on the throne of the beast, and its kingdom was plunged into darkness. People gnawed their tongues in anguish and cursed the God of heaven for their pain and sores. **They did not repent of their deeds."** – Revelation 16:8-11 ESV (Author's emphasis)

These passages indicate that repentance is clearly *still possible* during the Great Tribulation, before Christ's Second Coming and His millennial reign. Therefore, we must hope that there will be some who will be convicted of their rebellion during that horrendous time and will repent and trust in Jesus for their salvation.

In the next chapter, we are going to look at the rest of the Book of Revelation where we will see the scale of God's wrath intensifying. All who are left on the earth (after the Bride of Christ has been taken out of the world), will be faced with all that God's Word says concerning this terrifying time of trial. This will be so frightening, the mere reading of these passages of scripture ought to cause everyone who claims to be a follower of Christ to seriously examine their life to ensure they are living in accordance with His holy Word. Where we are sinning, we need to confess and repent of it, and receive His forgiveness and cleansing, as promised in the following passage;

"If we say we have no sin, we deceive ourselves, and the truth is not in us. If we confess our sins, he is faithful and just to forgive us our sins and to cleanse us from all unrighteousness." – 1 John 1:8-9 ESV

As a follower of Christ, surely, in the depths of our being, we must yearn to be counted among those who are worthy to escape what is coming upon the earth.

"But take heed to yourselves, lest your hearts be weighed down with carousing, drunkenness, and cares of this life, and that Day come on you unexpectedly. For it will come as a snare on all those who dwell on the face of the whole earth. Watch therefore, and pray always that **you may be counted worthy to escape all these things that will come to pass, and to stand before the Son of Man.**"
– Luke 21:34-36 NKJV (Author's emphasis)

Let's now move into the most dramatic part of the Book of Revelation; the time of the Great Tribulation. Let us study this next chapter with reverential fear and trembling for what the Lord will reveal to us.

Chapter 6

THE GREAT TRIBULATION, JESUS' SECOND COMING AND THE END OF THE ANTICHRIST

"This is a revelation from Jesus Christ, which God gave
him to show his servants the events that must soon take
place. He sent an angel to present this revelation to his servant
John, who faithfully reported everything he saw. This
is his report of the word of God and the testimony of Jesus
Christ. God blesses the one who reads the words of this
prophecy to the church, and he blesses all who listen to
its message and obey what it says, for the time is near."
—Revelation 1:1–3 NLT

It has been my experience throughout almost 30 years of being a follower of Christ, that a huge majority of believers think that what is told in the Book of Revelation (known as the Apocalypse to those who are Roman Catholics) is either beyond understanding for mere mortal human beings, or it is a fictional horror story like many movies of a similar nature. I was one such person for the first 20 years of my life as a Christian.

Having finally woken up from my state of complacency, it is my desire to show you, as clearly as I can from scripture, all that the Antichrist will do during the Great Tribulation, preceding the Second Coming of Christ.

Firstly, I want to encourage you to read again the passage at the head of this chapter, and allow its power and authority to sink in. It says that God gave the revelation to His Son, Jesus Christ, so that Jesus could show us, His servants, what *must* soon take place. God revealed it to Jesus; then Jesus sent His angel to reveal it to the Apostle John who faithfully reported everything he saw. The passage states that this (all that is written in the Book of Revelation) is his report of the Word of God and the testimony of Jesus Christ.

This is an astounding passage of scripture with an amazing statement of its faithfulness. If we profess to be a follower of the Bridegroom, we truly should believe this revelation that Jesus is showing us and treat the entirety of what we are about to discover with reverential fear and awe of the holiness and justice of God.

As we saw in the previous chapter, the Book of Revelation is such a vital book about the End Time events, given by Jesus to the Apostle John. As with the previous chapter, I will either show the biblical text and/or give a summary of each of the chapters from Revelation 8 to 22, so that it appears as a continuous vision. But by no means does this imply that I am removing anything from the Book of Revelation (see Revelation 22:19). I simply want to highlight what Jesus is saying will happen at each event and then write my own thoughts on it which I offer as suggestions, indications, and possible representations.

However, what I write, I will do so humbly before God with a prayerful heart, trusting in His guidance to lead me, and His mercy and grace to forgive me if I am in error. I do not wish to offer my thoughts as fact; they are merely my thoughts, although I have taken much time in prayer about them. Each reader is free to study and research the things I offer, or to reject them. I encourage you to read the full Bible text for yourself in a version of the Bible that you find easy to understand. In this chapter, the version I have used to write my summaries is the New Living Translation.

Revelation chapters 8–22 are the written account of the Great

Tribulation period. The revelation Jesus gives to John is a graphic vision of the catastrophic, cataclysmic collapse of the whole world leading up to the final end of the world, His Second Coming and the ultimate end of the Antichrist.

We saw at the end of our previous chapter that, in Revelation chapter 7, the 144,000 servants of the Lord will be sealed with God's protection to go out and preach the Gospel during the Great Tribulation, and that a vision is then given to John of the raptured believers standing before the throne of God.

Now we are at the critical point where Jesus opens the seventh seal which begins the time of the Great Tribulation.

So, let's enter into the vision and see what befalls those who are left on the earth after the Church has been redeemed.

Revelation 8: The Seventh Seal

Verse 1

John sees the Lamb open the seventh seal, and there is silence in heaven for about half an hour.

Initial comment: Before I continue, I would like to say something about that short but immensely powerful opening verse. Heaven is a place of endless worship to God by all the host of heaven—the angels, the elders, the four living creatures, all the faithful in the Old Testament, and now including the multitude of the raptured believers clothed in white. The moment that Jesus opens the seventh seal, which contains the final judgements of the seven trumpets, all of heaven falls silent.

Can you imagine just how serious and catastrophic these judgements will be if the opening of the seal that will commence these events causes the whole of heaven to fall into total silence for even one second, let alone half an hour? Whatever the Lamb is about to unveil with the opening of the seventh seal, all of heaven ceases its worship of God for half an hour, as they wait in complete silence for the seven trumpet judgements to unfold. The knowledge of this ought to make us shudder in reverential fear of what is about to come upon the earth.

Summary – Verses 2–5

> John sees the seven angels of God standing before Him and they are given seven trumpets. He sees another angel with a gold incense burner who stands at the altar. This angel is given a great amount of incense to mix with the prayers of God's holy people as an offering on the gold altar. The smoke of the incense mixed with the prayers of God's holy people rises up to God. This angel then fills the incense burner with fire from the altar and throws it down upon the earth. There is thunder, lightning, and a great earthquake.

Revelation 8:6–13: The First Four Trumpets

The following is the actual biblical text.

"Then the seven angels with the seven trumpets prepared to blow their mighty blasts.

The first angel blew his trumpet, and hail and fire mixed with blood were thrown down on the earth. One-third of the earth was set on fire, one-third of the trees were burned, and all the green grass was burned.

Then the second angel blew his trumpet, and a great mountain of fire was thrown into the sea. One-third of the water in the sea became blood, one-third of all things living in the sea died, and one-third of all the ships on the sea were destroyed.

Then the third angel blew his trumpet, and a great star fell from the sky, burning like a torch. It fell on one-third of the rivers and on the springs of water. The name of the star was Bitterness. It made one-third of the water bitter, and many people died from drinking the bitter water.

Then the fourth angel blew his trumpet, and one-third of the sun was struck, and one-third of the moon, and one third of the stars, and they became dark. And one-third of the day was dark, and also one-third of the night.

Then I looked, and I heard a single eagle crying loudly as it flew through the air, "Terror, terror, terror to all who belong to this world because of what will happen when the last three angels blow their trumpets." —Revelation 8:6–13 NLT

(The literal meaning in the Greek for the star named Bitterness is 'wormwood.')

Revelation 9: The Fifth and Sixth Trumpets

The fifth trumpet

The following is the actual biblical text.

"Then the fifth angel blew his trumpet, and I saw a star that had fallen to earth from the sky, and he was given the key to the shaft of the bottomless pit. When he opened it, smoke poured out as though from a huge furnace, and the sunlight and air turned dark from the smoke.

Then locusts came from the smoke and descended on the earth, and they were given power to sting like scorpions. They were told not to harm the grass or plants or trees, but only the people who did not have the seal of God on their foreheads. They were told not to kill them but to torture them for five months with pain like the pain of a scorpion sting. In those days people will seek death but will not find it. They will long to die, but death will flee from them!

The locusts looked like horses prepared for battle. They had what looked like gold crowns on their heads, and their faces looked like human faces. They had hair like women's hair and teeth like the teeth of a lion. They wore armor made of iron, and their wings roared like an army of chariots rushing into battle. They had tails that stung like scorpions, and for five months they had the power to torment people. Their king is the angel from the bottomless pit; his name in Hebrew is Abaddon, and in Greek, Apollyon—the Destroyer.

The first terror is past, but look, two more terrors are coming!" – Revelation 9:1–12 NLT

(The bottomless pit is also known as the abyss or the underworld.)

The sixth trumpet

The following is the actual biblical text.

"Then the sixth angel blew his trumpet, and I heard a voice speaking from the four horns of the gold altar that stands in the presence of God. And the voice said to the sixth angel who held the trumpet, "Release the four angels who are bound at the great Euphrates River." Then the four angels who had been prepared for this hour and day and month and year were turned loose to kill one-third of all the people on earth. I heard the size of their army, which was 200 million mounted troops.

And in my vision, I saw the horses and the riders sitting on them. The riders wore armor that was fiery red and dark blue and yellow. The horses had heads like lions, and fire and smoke and burning sulfur billowed from their mouths. One third of all the people on earth were killed by these three plagues—by the fire and smoke and burning sulfur that came from the mouths of the horses. Their power was in their mouths and in their tails. For their tails had heads like snakes, with the power to injure people.

But the people who did not die in these plagues still

refused to repent of their evil deeds and turn to God. They continued to worship demons and idols made of gold, silver, bronze, stone, and wood—idols that can neither see nor hear nor walk! And they did not repent of their murders or their witchcraft or their sexual immorality or their thefts." – Revelation 9:13–21 NLT

My comments: The detail in chapter 9 is very descriptive, but if we simplify it for the sake of clarity, it will help us to see through all the description. Let's look at the text again.

At the beginning of Revelation 9, it tells us of the star that had fallen. This is in the past tense so refers to a star that *had* fallen before the vision was given. Remember, Satan was previously an angel known as Lucifer or 'morning star', and he was cast down to earth when he rebelled and tried to exalt himself above God. Satan took with him a multitude of angels who also rebelled against God and they were all cast down to earth (see Isaiah 14:12–15). So, the star that was *"given the key to the shaft of the Abyss"* (see Revelation 9:1) could be a fallen angel or even Satan himself. The Abyss is hell. We are then told of the locusts that will come out of the Abyss to torture and torment those who are left on earth, for five months. These would be unbelievers, and those in the apostasy - the great Falling Away - who once believed but then abandoned their faith in Jesus and rejected His Word. It would also include complacent Christians who thought they were ready for the return of the Bridegroom but whose hearts and lives demonstrated that they loved the ways of the godless world more than they yearned for Him.

What is shocking is that, despite all of the horrors that occur in the events of the fifth and sixth trumpet judgements, it will not cause them to fall on their faces before God in repentance of all their sin.

If we are a believer and are involved in habitual sin which we casually dismiss or proudly claim is our right to practice, if we have refused to confess and repent of it *prior* to Jesus coming to rapture the Church, we could find ourselves left on the earth to endure this horror.

Revelation 10: The Angel and the Scroll

Summary – Verses 1–7

John sees another mighty angel descend from heaven with a scroll in his hand. When the angel gave a loud shout the voice of seven thunders spoke. John was about to write down what the seven thunders spoke, but a voice from heaven told him not to do this and said that what the seven thunders spoke must be sealed up. The mighty angel with the scroll lifts his right hand to heaven and declares that there will be no more delay and that when the seventh trumpet is sounded, the mysterious plan of God will be accomplished and fulfilled just as He had announced to His servants the prophets.

Summary – Verses 8-11

The voice from heaven instructs John to take the scroll (which contains the sealed words of the seven thunders) out of the mighty angel's hand. He is told to eat the scroll, which will be sweet in the mouth but turn sour in the stomach. John is told to prophesy *again* about many people, nations, languages, and kings.

My comments: Whatever the prophetic words of the seven thunders are on the scroll, we can assume that this scroll contains very serious words of judgement for all the people of the world, in view of the effect it has on him physically when he consumes it.

Revelation 11: The Two Witnesses

Summary – Verses 1-14

John is shown that for 3½ years the Holy City (Jerusalem) will be trampled on by the Gentile nations. At this time, two End Times witnesses will appear who will prophesy for 1,260 days (i.e. the 3½ years). During this time, they will have power to withhold the rain, turn water into blood, and strike the earth with every kind of plague as often as they want. If anyone tries to harm them, fire will come out of their mouths to destroy their enemies. At the end of the 3½ years when they finish prophesying, the beast will come out of the Abyss to kill them. Their bodies will lie in the street of the great city for 3½ days and will not be permitted burial. People from every nation, tribe, and language will come and gaze at their bodies and gloat over them and even celebrate their death by giving presents to each other, because God's two witnesses 'tormented' them with their prophesying. Suddenly, at the end of the 3½ days, God will bring them back to life and they will stand up. Terror will strike everyone who sees this. Then a loud voice from heaven will call the two witnesses up and they will ascend in a cloud while their enemies look on. (I referred to this specific 'Rapture' event earlier under the sub-heading 'The Question of the Rapture'). At that very hour the city will be hit by a severe earthquake causing a tenth of it to collapse, and seven thousand people will die. The survivors will be terrified, but they will give glory to God.

My comments: It would seem that some people's hearts will be turned to God at this point.

Summary – Verses 15-19: The Seventh Trumpet

This is the final trumpet judgement. As the angel sounds his trumpet, loud voices are heard in heaven declaring that the kingdom of the world (which became Satan's kingdom after he was cast out of heaven and down to earth because of his rebellion against God; see Isaiah 14:12–15) has now become the kingdom of God and of Christ, who will reign forever and ever. The twenty-four elders, who are sitting on their thrones, fall on their faces and worship God, proclaiming that the time has come for judging the dead; for rewarding God's servants, the prophets, the saints, and those who revere God's name; and for destroying those who cause destruction on the earth. Then John sees God's temple in heaven open and also sees the Ark of the Covenant. Again, there is lightning, rumbling, thunder, an earthquake and a great hailstorm.

Revelation 12: The Woman and the Dragon

Initial comments: From this chapter onwards we each need to ask the Lord for further wisdom in understanding the various descriptions and symbolism used throughout the text. Many believers get put off and give up trying to understand it or even stop reading the Book of Revelation altogether. It has taken me a long time to get to the point of asking the Lord to help me make sense of it. If we prayerfully seek the Lord to give us words that could be used in place of the symbolic words, it will become much easier to understand. I have done this and have used the words that I feel the Lord has given me which could represent the symbolism used in these further chapters of the Book of Revelation.

So that readers do not get completely baffled, below is a list of the existing biblical symbols, and next to them I have written some up-to-date representations that could apply:

- Woman – The nation of Israel and the Church (both Gentile and Jewish followers of Christ), and Mary (the mother of Jesus).
- Child – Jesus.
- Offspring – True followers of Christ (both Gentile & Jewish believers).
- Dragon – Satan.
- First beast – Global leader (the Antichrist).

- Second beast – The false prophet (assistant to the first beast).

- Seven heads – Seven leaders within the global 7-nation alliance (before it becomes ten).

- Ten horns – The ten nations which make up the final global alliance, ruled by the global leader (the Antichrist).

- Ten crowns – Indicating that the ten horns are the ten kingdoms.

- Saints (in Revelation 13) – Those who repent and turn to Christ during the Great Tribulation.

- Scarlet beast – Global alliance and its leader (the Antichrist).

- The woman on the scarlet beast – The great prostitute/ religious organization.

- Lamb – Jesus.

For some current information which may help with our understanding of the symbolism of the seven heads and the ten horns, the current G7 group of nations is soon to become the G10 alliance of ten nations. This seems fascinating if we are truly near the End Times formation of the New World Order.

So, as we proceed to my summaries of the remainder of the Book of Revelation, I will either insert the above up-to-date words next to the existing symbolic words or I will write my thoughts throughout the text to offer possibilities as to what the text could mean. As there are varying views on End Times prophecy, I would encourage you to research Bible commentaries on all of the remaining chapters of the Book of Revelation.

Summary of Revelation 12

John is given a vision of a 'woman' clothed with the sun, with the moon at her feet, a crown of twelve stars on her head, and a dragon at her feet ready to devour her 'Child'. This Child was caught up to God and His throne.

The dragon (Satan), having not succeeded in devouring the woman's Child (Jesus) then proceeds to go after her 'offspring' (all true believers).

My comments: There are several schools of thought concerning this 'woman'. Many suggest this is Mary, the mother of Jesus, because the vision shows that the dragon was ready to devour her Child (Jesus), but He was caught up to God and His throne. As we know, Satan (the dragon) tried to devour Mary's Child at the Cross, but after His death and resurrection, He was caught up to heaven (His ascension) to be with God and is now seated at the right hand of the throne of God (see Mark 16:19).

Others believe this vision of a 'woman' represents the Church, and also the nation of Israel in view of the twelve stars on her crown which could be symbolic of the twelve tribes of Israel. It is vital that we understand that the Church consists of both Gentile *and* Jewish followers of Christ.

The woman's Child is undoubtedly Jesus as there is no other person who is at God's throne except Jesus. The woman's 'offspring' could additionally represent all believers down through the ages and those (both Jewish and Gentile) in the future who follow Jesus Christ, obey the Word of God, and keep their testimony to the end. Satan hates the woman's 'offspring' (all true believers) who have put their faith in Jesus Christ for their salvation, and his persecution of believers will continue until Christ's Second Coming when Satan will be thrown into the lake of fire.

For a commentary on Revelation 12, visit https://lifehopeandtruth.com/prophecy/revelation/revelation-12/

Revelation 13:1–18: The Two Beasts and the Mark

Summary – Verses 1-2

John sees a beast with seven heads, ten horns, and ten crowns on its horns rising up out of the sea. On each of the seven heads are names that blaspheme God. The dragon gives this beast his power and his throne and great authority. This beast has the power and the throne of Satan.

My comments: As the angel was giving John a vision of things to come - *future events* which would occur at the time of the end - we must look at these prophetic visions on this basis. This 'beast' could represent the global leader (who will be the Antichrist) of an alliance of nations which has immense authority over the whole world. Its 'heads' (leaders) are against God, as indicated by their blasphemies. It seems to suggest an authority that is made up of seven nations but will become ten nations. The fact that each has a crown suggests that these are sovereign nations; a group of ten 'kingdoms' creating a new global superpower alliance.

Verse 3(a)

In the vision, one of the seven heads (leaders) has a wound, which appears fatal but is then healed.

My comments: This could suggest that one of the leaders of the 7-nation alliance is fatally wounded at some point, but is healed. Another possibility is that perhaps the actual *nation* (of which this leader is the head), will be overthrown (i.e. fatally wounded) but will then be revived again (healed).

Summary – Verses 3(b)-7(a)

Because of this 'healing', the whole world will marvel at it, and this will cause the world to follow this beast (global leader). Because the dragon (Satan) gives the first beast (the global leader/Antichrist) *his* power, the people worship both the dragon and the beast. This beast (global leader/Antichrist), with authority over the world, will speak proud and blasphemous words for 3½ years against God, against heaven, and against those who dwell in heaven, and will use his power and authority to wage war against God's holy people and to conquer them.

My comments: The holy people here are those who have become followers of Christ *during* the Great Tribulation, and also the Jewish people who are still on the earth because of their continued rejection of Jesus Christ as their Messiah.

A quick reminder here that the 144,000 servants of the Lord from the twelve tribes of Israel are sealed by God to preach the Gospel to the Jews *during* the Great Tribulation, in a final attempt to show them that Jesus Christ is their Messiah, and to bring them to faith in Him for their salvation.

Summary – Verses 7(b)-12

The beast (global leader/Antichrist) will be so powerful that his satanic authority will rule over every tribe and people and language and nation. All the people who belong to this world (those who refuse to believe in Jesus Christ) will worship the beast (global leader/Antichrist). Their names are *not* written in the Book of Life, which belongs to the Lamb that was slain (Jesus). The saints (those who repent and come to Christ *during* the Great Tribulation) are called to patient endurance and faithfulness during this horrific time.

A second beast (the false prophet) will then appear, coming up out of the earth, and will exercise all authority on behalf of the first beast (the global leader/Antichrist of the alliance of ten nations).

My comments: We know the second beast is the false prophet because this is confirmed in Revelation 16:13, 19:20 and 20:10. I just want to point out that a false prophet is a person who *claims* to represent God on the earth, sitting in a position of authority to speak on behalf of God to the people. His words will sound pleasant and soothing but will be contrary to the Word of God, being subtly twisted so as to deceive the masses. The End Times false prophet will be someone who is powerful, esteemed by the world as a true 'man of God' who holds sway over all the nations. World leaders, as well as the general public, will give this person respect and honour, and bow down before him whether they believe in God or not.

Revelation chapter 13 clearly indicates that the Antichrist leader and this powerful 'man of God' (false prophet) will work together, but the Antichrist leader will 'pull all the strings' whilst the false prophet carries out the commands given to him.

Summary – Verses 13-15

The false prophet will force all the people to worship the global leader/Antichrist, and will perform great signs and miracles on behalf of the Antichrist, thereby deceiving the whole world to worship and follow him. The false prophet will order a statue to be made of the Antichrist leader *and will give this statue life so that it can speak.* This 'living' statue of the global leader will order that anyone who does not worship it must die.

My comments: This is intriguing. What could possibly make a *statue* come to life and speak? With Artificial Intelligence (AI) technology that exists today, being created by some very powerful people who have global influence, the creation of human-like robots that are 'alive' and are able to communicate, is already happening. It is highly possible that AI technology could be used to enable this statue of the Antichrist leader to appear alive and have the ability to speak.

Summary – Verses 16-17: The Mark of the Beast

The second beast (false prophet), who represents the first beast (Antichrist leader), will then force everyone - from the least to the greatest, rich and poor, slave and free - to be given a mark on their right hand or on their forehead so that no one can buy or sell anything *unless* they have the mark. This mark is the name of the beast (Antichrist leader) or the number representing his name.

My comments: Remember, Satan has given the Antichrist leader his power and authority. Therefore, if you receive the mark of the beast, it means you belong to Satan. Scripture exhorts us to use wisdom to solve the meaning of the number of the beast (the Antichrist)—the number of a man whose number is 666. In the Greek and Roman alphabet, each letter has a numerical equivalent. You can use this numerical system to work out the number of your own name. You can use it to work out the number of all of Jesus' names and also the number of all of Satan's names. Therefore, we must not be afraid to use technology in our search for information on this matter. It may reveal some information that could help us unravel the mysteries of all of this.

Verse 18

> "Wisdom is needed here. Let the one with understanding **solve the meaning of the number of the beast,** for it is the number of a man. His number is 666" – NLT translation (Author's emphasis).

My comments: This is an instruction from the Lord which we need to heed and carry out. Using the Greek and Roman numerical system, our search should look for a man, or the *name* of a man who represents a system of political and religious authority that embraces the whole world. The subject of the mark of the beast should not be scoffed at. It will become a reality. If God should decide to send Jesus to Rapture the true believers in *our* lifetime, then this would mean that the period of the Great Tribulation would immediately follow in our lifetime too. The scriptures show that implementation of the mark of the beast will occur during this period.

This being the case, as we have seen previously, there would have to be a slow and subtle preparation to produce and test various prototypes of the 'mark' on the unsuspecting world that will eventually be placed on the forehead or the right hand. This preparation would have to take place in the time period *prior* to the commencement of the Great Tribulation.

This preparation could be taking place right now while we go about our daily business, unaware of how Satan is using his earthly followers, including high-powered leaders, to fulfil this devastating part of End Times prophecy. It has to happen at some point before the Great Tribulation begins, so it could easily be happening right now, and from what we have seen in previous chapters, it most probably is.

Revelation 14: The Lamb and the 144,000, the Three Angels, and the Harvests

Summary – Verses 1-5: The Lamb and the 144,000

John is then shown a vision of the 144,000 from the twelve tribes of Israel who have now clearly been taken into heaven after completing their work for the Lord during the Great Tribulation. These specially chosen servants of the Lord are the ones who have kept themselves as pure as virgins, have never lied, and are blameless. They have the name of God, the name of the Lamb, and the seal of God on their foreheads, and they will stand with the Lamb on Mount Zion. A great choir of angels sings a wonderful new song in front of God's throne and only these 144,000 are able to learn it. They follow the Lamb wherever He goes. They have been *redeemed from the earth* (raptured) as a special offering to God and to the Lamb.

My comments: As I mentioned in Chapter 5, it would appear that the Lord raptures them separately out of the Great Tribulation.

Summary – Verses 6-7: The Three Angels

John then sees three angels making proclamations. The first angel proclaims the eternal Gospel to all the peoples of every nation, tribe, and language, telling them to fear God and give Him glory because the hour of God's judgement has come.

My comments: This is very interesting. Remember we saw in Chapter 4 that Jesus said the Gospel must be preached in every nation and then the end will come (see Matthew 24:14). For some reason, Christians on the earth today seem to think that we are supposed to completely fulfil this Great Commission *before* the Church is raptured. However, from what John is shown in this vision, clearly the preaching of the Gospel to all nations is still being carried out *during* the Great Tribulation by one of God's angels! This is fascinating but equally sobering; at this critical point, God is even using one of His holy angels to proclaim the Gospel of salvation to those left behind on the earth because, in His great mercy, the Lord does not want anyone to perish (see 2 Peter 3:9) and He is giving the whole of humanity one last opportunity to repent of their sins and put their faith in Jesus Christ to save them.

Summary – Verses 8-12

> The second angel declares that Babylon has fallen; the great city that made all the nations drink the wine of her adulteries (we will see the description of Babylon later, in Revelation 17). The third angel declares that if anyone worships the beast (Antichrist leader) and his statue, and receives his mark on their hand or forehead, they will also receive the wrath of God which has been poured out full strength into His cup of wrath. They will be tormented with burning sulphur in the presence of the holy angels and the Lamb, and the smoke of their torment will rise forever and ever. There is no rest day or night for those who worship the Antichrist leader and his statue, or for anyone who receives the mark of his name. Those who are God's children, who obey God's commandments and remain faithful to Jesus, must patiently endure this horrific time. This third angel is confirming what was shown to John in Revelation chapter 13.

My comments: As I have mentioned throughout this book, I believe the reference to the children of God mentioned at this point relates to people who become followers of Christ *during* the Great Tribulation, together with all those who had previously professed to be believers but were not ready when Jesus returned to Rapture the Church. Having been left behind, it seems that some will come to their senses during the Great Tribulation and repent of their sin and turn back to believing and following Jesus prior to His Second Coming. It is these 'Tribulation saints' who will be faced with the choice of taking the mark of the beast in order to survive, or to refuse it and face death. The Church saints (those who are raptured before the wrath of God begins) will not be on the earth, so this issue does not concern them. It is vital that anyone who comes to Christ during the Great Tribulation *does not* receive the mark of the beast (the Antichrist's mark), as receiving it will mean that they will then belong to Satan. Any profession of still being a Christian will be overridden by the Antichrist's mark which they have accepted.

Verse 13

John then hears a voice from heaven that tells him to write down these words:

"…Blessed are those who die in the Lord from now on. Yes, says the Spirit, they are blessed indeed, for they will rest from their hard work; for their good deeds will follow them!" (Revelation 14.13 NLT).

My comments: This could indicate that from that point on, anyone who is a believer or becomes a believer during the Great Tribulation may be put to death as a result of their faith in the Lord.

Summary – The Two Harvests

Verse 14

John sees that two harvests then take place. The first harvest is carried out by a person on a white cloud who appears like the Son of Man with a gold crown on His head. An angel from the temple of God calls to Him loudly to swing the sharp sickle in His hand and reap the harvest of the earth because the time has come.

My comments: This would seem to be Jesus undertaking the final gathering of all the previously lukewarm, complacent believers (who had been left behind on earth at the Rapture), who have now repented, plus any unbelievers (both Jewish and Gentile) who have turned to Him during the Great Tribulation. This is the Rapture of the Tribulation saints. At the completion of this harvest, it is quite sobering to realise that every true believer is now safely with the Lord; the Old Testament believers (before Christ's first coming), the Church believers, the 144,000 Jewish servants of the Lord, the two End Time witnesses, and now finally the Tribulation saints.

Verses 15-20

The second harvest is carried out by an angel who comes out of the temple, also holding a sharp sickle in his hand. Another angel calls loudly to this angel to take his sickle and gather the clusters of grapes from the *earth's* vine (i.e. the people on earth who refuse to believe in Jesus). The angel does this and throws the grapes of this harvest into the winepress of God's wrath where they will be trampled in the winepress outside the city. Their blood will flow out of the press rising up to the height of a horse's bridle for a distance of 180 miles.

My comments: This is not some fictional horror story. It is a real horror story that is *really* going to happen. This angel would seem to be the 'grim reaper' who comes to destroy all those who have not believed in God or His Son, Jesus Christ. We will see what wrath they have to experience in the following summaries of chapters 15 and 16.

Revelation 15: The Seven Angels with the Seven Plagues

Initial comments: After all that has occurred so far, things intensify even more on the earth, which now has only unbelievers and also unrepentant believers left on it (after the final gathering up of the remaining repentant believers in Revelation 14). The following events, which I believe are the winepress of God's wrath mentioned in the previous section, are the final things that will be happening on the earth right up to the end of the world.

Summary – Verses 1-4

John sees seven angels with the last seven plagues. These are the last plagues because they are the final acts of God's wrath upon all those who refuse to believe in His Son, Jesus Christ, (as we shall see next in Revelation 16). But before the angels pour out these plagues, John sees all those who have been victorious over the beast and his statue and over the number representing his name. They are standing beside a sea that looks like glass mixed with fire. They hold harps that God has given them, and they sing the song of Moses and the song of the Lamb.

My comments: I believe this is a vision of all the final Tribulation saints who we saw were gathered up (raptured) in the first harvest in the previous section relating to Revelation chapter 14.

Summary – Verses 5-8

After this, John sees the temple of God opened, and out of the temple come the seven angels dressed in clean, shining linen with golden sashes around their chests. One of the four living creatures gives the seven angels the seven bowls filled with the wrath of God (the last seven plagues). The temple is filled with smoke from the glory of God and from His power. No one can enter the temple until the seven plagues are completed.

Revelation 16: The Last Seven Plagues

Summary – Verses 1-21

John hears a loud voice from the temple telling the seven angels to pour out the seven bowls of God's wrath. The first angel pours out his bowl onto the earth. Painful, ugly sores break out on everyone who has the mark of the beast and who worships his image. The second angel pours out his bowl onto the sea and it turns into blood, and every living thing in the sea dies. The third angel pours out his bowl on the rivers and springs of water and they turn to blood too. John then hears the angel, who is in charge of the waters, say,

"...You are just, O Holy One, who is and who always was, because you have sent these judgments.
Since they shed the blood
of your holy people and your prophets,
you have given them blood to drink.
It is their just reward."

And I heard a voice from the altar, saying,

"Yes, O Lord God, the Almighty,
your judgments are true and just." – Revelation 16:5(b)-7 NLT.

The fourth angel pours out his bowl on the sun, and it is given power to scorch people with fire. They curse the name of God who has control over these plagues, *but they refuse to repent of their sins and give glory to God.* The fifth angel pours out his bowl on the throne of the beast (global leader/Antichrist), and his kingdom is plunged into darkness. The people gnaw their tongues in agony because of their pains and their sores, *but still they refuse to repent of what they have done.*

The sixth angel pours out his bowl on the great river Euphrates, and its waters dry up to prepare the way for the kings from the East to come for the final battle at the place called Armageddon. Three evil spirits that look like frogs, come out of the mouth of the dragon (Satan) and out of the mouth of the beast (global leader/Antichrist) and out of the mouth of the false prophet. These evil frog-like spirits are demons that perform miraculous signs, and they go out to the kings of the whole world to gather them for the battle on the great day of God Almighty.

Once the kings of the earth are gathered at the place called Armageddon, the seventh angel pours out his bowl into the air, and a loud voice comes out of the temple from the throne saying, *"It is finished!"* Then there is lightning and rumbling, the like of which has never occurred since man has been on the earth. The great city (Babylon) splits into three sections, and the cities of the nations collapse into heaps of rubble. God remembers Babylon's sins and makes her drink the cup of the wine of His fierce wrath. All the islands disappear, and the mountains are levelled. Huge hailstones, each weighing about a hundred pounds, fall from the sky upon the people and they curse God because this plague is so terrible.

My comments: God's Word has said all these things *will* happen, therefore we need to believe it. Remember, it is Jesus Himself who gave the revelation to His angel to show the Apostle John what is going to happen. Bearing this in mind, God has also said to us in His Word, "…This is my dearly loved Son, who brings me great joy. **Listen to Him.**" – Matthew 17:5(b) NLT (Author's emphasis)

Revelation 17: The Great Prostitute

Summary – Verses 1-7(a)

One of the seven angels shows John the judgement that

is going to come upon the 'great prostitute' who rules over many waters. The kings of the earth have committed adultery with this great prostitute and the people of the earth are intoxicated with the wine of her adulteries. The angel shows John a woman sitting on a scarlet beast that has seven heads and ten horns and it has blasphemies against God all over it (the same beast and the same horns mentioned in Revelation chapter 13). This woman (the great prostitute) is dressed in purple and scarlet and has jewellery of gold and precious gems and pearls (again mentioned in Revelation 13). In her hand is a golden cup filled with abominable things and the filth of her adulteries. On this woman's forehead is written a name that is a mystery, 'Babylon the Great, the Mother of Prostitutes and of the Abominations of the Earth'. (Note: This 'woman' is not the 'woman' mentioned in Revelation chapter 12).

This woman is drunk with the blood of the saints, those who bear testimony of Jesus. The beast (that the woman sits upon) murders and has murdered true believers, probably many millions throughout the centuries. John is astonished at what he is seeing, and so the angel of the Lord explains to him the mystery of the woman and the beast she is sitting on.

Below is the biblical text of the remainder of Revelation 17, verses 7(b)-18 NLT

"I will tell you the mystery of this woman and of the beast with seven heads and ten horns on which she sits. The beast you saw was once alive but isn't now. And yet he will soon come up out of the bottomless pit and go to eternal destruction. And the people who belong to this world, whose names were not written in the Book of Life before the world was made, will be amazed at the reappearance of this beast who had died.

"This calls for a mind with understanding: The seven heads of the beast represent the seven hills where the woman rules. They also represent seven kings. Five kings have already fallen, the sixth now reigns, and the seventh is yet to come, but his reign will be brief.

"The scarlet beast that was, but is no longer, is the eighth king. He is like the other seven, and he, too, is headed for destruction. The ten horns of the beast are ten kings who have not yet risen to power. They will be appointed to their kingdoms for one brief moment to reign with the beast. They will all agree to give him their power and authority. Together they will go to war against the Lamb, but the Lamb will defeat them because he is Lord of all lords and King of all kings. And his called and chosen and faithful ones will be with him."

Then the angel said to me, "The waters where the prostitute is ruling represent masses of people of every nation and language. The scarlet beast and his ten horns all hate the prostitute. They will strip her naked, eat her flesh, and burn her remains with fire. For God has put a plan into their minds, a plan that will carry out his purposes. They will agree to give their authority to the scarlet beast, and so the words of God will be fulfilled. And this woman you saw in your vision represents the great city that rules over the kings of the world."

My comments: Let's try and unpack this: I will start with the woman referred to as 'the great prostitute'. Right at the end of the above passage, the angel says that this woman is *the great city* that rules over the kings of the earth. The word *woman* is often used to refer to the Church or a *religious system*. The true Church of believers is known as the Bride of Christ. But this woman, known as the great prostitute, could indicate a religious organization that appears to be in the form of the Church, which outwardly looks godly and appears to be following Christ, thereby attracting and deceiving many people from all nations, tribes, and languages. But inwardly its root is not in Christ at all but belongs to the dragon (Satan).

This religious organization may use the words *God, Jesus Christ* and *Holy Spirit,* and may outwardly go through the religious motions, but nonetheless it is a deception. Remember, Satan's purpose is to deceive the whole world into following him, and what better way to do it than produce a counterfeit form of Christianity; something that looks like the Church and displays a form of holiness and godliness. Satan is not going to make it obvious to the world that it is he who is deceiving them. A deception is something that looks like the authentic thing but in fact is a fake. Think of counterfeit money; sometimes fake money is so well produced that even the experts are fooled into believing it is the real thing. This is what Satan is doing by creating a global religious organization that looks like authentic Christianity but is in fact a counterfeit.

The great prostitute/religious organization is sitting on the scarlet beast (the global 10-nation alliance ruled by the global leader/Antichrist). The words 'sitting on' indicate that this religious organization rules over, or is in control of the 'kings' of this global alliance. This great prostitute/religious organization wears purple and scarlet clothing and is decked with gold, silver, precious stones and pearls, and holds a gold goblet in her hand.

The angel of the Lord states that the 'waters' where this great prostitute/religious organization sits (rules) are actually the masses of peoples of every nation and language. This religious organization rules over a vast majority of peoples from all nations of the world.

We need to remember that this is a prophecy concerning the End Times period that was being shown to the Apostle John in a vision - a vision that would be fulfilled at an appointed time long after John's death, and would refer to nations, kingdoms, peoples and situations that had not yet occurred at the time the vision was given to him.

The angel of the Lord describes the scarlet beast as 'someone' (or a regime) that was once alive but had died (or no longer in existence), yet will soon be revived. The people of the world, whose names are *not* written in the Book of Life, will be amazed at the reappearance of this beast (the global alliance). We saw this previously in the summary for Revelation chapter 13. Many scholars believe this will be the revived Roman Empire consisting of a 10-nation alliance of nations.

The angel says that the seven heads of the scarlet beast represent the seven hills where the woman (religious organization) rules. This beast rules from its 'headquarters' among seven hills. These seven heads also represent kings (or people in positions of authority over the religious organization). Five had already been and gone at the time this vision was given to John, the sixth was reigning, and the seventh was yet to come and would reign for only a brief period. After the seventh king has had his brief reign, the scarlet beast (the global alliance) that was once alive but had died, will be revived and become the eighth (and final) king (kingdom) that will rule the world.

This indicates this final global leader will take over from the previous heads. Each of these heads, in succession, fulfils a role on the earth with great power and authority over multitudes of peoples from all the nations of the earth. The angel says that this scarlet beast (the global alliance) *"is headed for destruction"*.

The angel says, *"This calls for a mind with understanding"*. All that is written in Revelation 17 is very complicated. I do not pretend to know what this all means, but from my research, many Bible scholars seem to concur with what I have written.

The angel says that this woman *is sitting on* the scarlet beast with the ten horns. Again, we could interpret the phrase as meaning that the woman (the religious organization) is 'ruling' the beast (the global alliance). The religious organization that rules the whole world is in control of the global alliance which is made up of ten kingdoms.

If we refer back to my summary of Revelation chapter 13, we will see that the ten horns could refer to ten kingdoms with ten kings represented by the ten crowns mentioned in Revelation 13:1. Indeed, in Revelation 17:12, God's Word confirms that the ten horns of the beast are ten kings who had not yet risen to power at the time that John was given this vision. The ten kings (ten nations) will rise to power and be appointed to their kingdoms for one brief moment to reign with the beast (as part of the global alliance). *All these ten kings will agree to give the beast their power and their authority.* This means that the leaders of the ten nations will give their sovereign power and authority to the global alliance to form a New World Order which will reign for one brief moment.

Have we grasped this? Ten kingdoms will suddenly join together for a brief time, giving all their power and authority to the beast (the global alliance with its global leader, the Antichrist) who is their head and rules over them. Whatever power and authority they have as individual kingdoms, they will just agree to give this over to him! The purpose of this is so that the beast (Antichrist) will use his great authority over the world and, together with the ten horns (the ten nations who have given him their power and authority) will go to war against the Lamb (Jesus). But the Lamb will defeat them because He is the Lord of all lords and the King of all kings, and His chosen and faithful ones will be with Him. We will see this battle take place at Armageddon, as described further ahead in Revelation 19.

As we have seen, the woman (the religious organization) who wears the purple and scarlet clothing, sits on (rules over) the beast (the global alliance with the Antichrist as its leader). Even though the Antichrist leader has been given Satan's power and authority (see Revelation 13:2), it would seem that the religious organization is the seat of this satanic power despite its outward appearance of holiness and godliness.

The beast and his ten horns (the global alliance of ten nations) actually all hate this woman (the satanic great prostitute/religious organization) who it seems ultimately controls them, and so they will strip her naked, eat her flesh, and burn her remains with fire. God has actually put this plan into their minds to carry out the fulfilment of His purposes, and we will look at this next in Revelation 18.

For further commentary on this, visit https://lifehopeandtruth.com/prophecy/revelation/revelation-17/

Revelation 18: The Fall of Babylon

Summary – Verses 1-13

Now we come to the destruction of this great prostitute/ religious organization. John is shown the graphic description of the fall and destruction of the 'great city' Babylon at the hand of God's wrath. It becomes a home for demons and every foul spirit and every foul and dreadful animal. This city exalted itself on its throne and all the nations fell because they grew rich due to this city's extravagant luxury. The nations of the world supplied everything that this city needed, and now it is brought to ruin, and all the nations mourn at its sudden destruction. As they see the smoke rise, they are terrified. The nations of the world supplied this city with great quantities of gold, silver, jewels, pearls, purple and scarlet cloth, silk, ivory goods, objects made from expensive wood, marble, bronze, iron, and many other things, *including human slaves.*

My comments: Again, research is needed. This city, which is involved in human trafficking, is the woman (religious organization) mentioned in Revelation 17, who is clothed in the finest purple and scarlet linen and decked with gold, silver, precious stones, and pearls. But the city's destruction has come. In a single moment it is all gone, and the world looks on in astonishment. This city deceived the nations with its sorceries or trickeries.

Verse 20

> John sees that the people of God, the apostles, and the whole of heaven are told to rejoice over the destruction of this city, for at last God has judged it for *their* sakes. This city will never be found again. It will cease to exist.

Verse 24

> The angel shows John that this city's streets flow with the blood of the prophets of God and of God's holy people, and the blood of people slaughtered all over the world.

My comments: God is going to utterly destroy this lying, deceiving religious organization forever for what it has done to the peoples and nations of this world.

So many people in 21st century Christianity think that this 'mystery Babylon' is a nation. What needs to be noted here is that God's Word says it is a *city*…not a nation. It is a city built on seven hills (as noted in Revelation 17:9), and most Bible scholars believe that this city is Rome.

Revelation 19: Shouting in Heaven and the White Horse Rider

Summary – Verses 1–9

> John then hears what sounds like a vast crowd in heaven shouting praises to the Lord for the destruction of this great city that corrupted the whole world with its immorality. The twenty-four elders and the four living creatures fall down and worship God. Then John hears more shouting in heaven, praising the Lord who reigns and exhorting us to *"…be glad and rejoice for the time has come for the wedding feast of the Lamb, **and his bride has prepared**

herself. She has been given the finest of pure white linen to wear." For the fine linen represents the good deeds of God's holy people.' (Verses 7–8 NLT, author's emphasis).

My comments: These good deeds are not only the good things we do, such as helping others, they are also the good deeds which we demonstrate in the way we live our life in Christ. The state of our heart, the thoughts of our mind, the words we speak, and our attitudes and motives - these all represent our deeds. If we examine our deeds, will we find them to be good or bad?

This is the long-awaited marriage of the Lamb of God (Jesus) with His Bride (all faithful, obedient believers). We have seen previously that those believers have already been redeemed from the earth and are in heaven, worshipping at the throne of God, but now we see them enter the final marriage feast.

'The angel of the Lord says, "…Blessed are those who are **invited** to the wedding feast of the Lamb…"' (Verse 9 NLT - author's emphasis).

This word 'invited' is very important and has been greatly overlooked in today's Church. God's Word tells us that not everyone will enter heaven when they die. Those who will be received and welcomed into heaven are *invited*. That invitation is from God. It is the Gospel message of salvation through faith in His Son, Jesus Christ, the Bridegroom to whom the invitation relates. God freely distributes this salvation wedding invitation to the whole of the human race from every nation, tribe, and language through the preaching and the witness of true followers of Jesus Christ. The invitation is given out, *but* just because you have received an invitation, it does not automatically give you the right to expect entry to the wedding. You have to *respond* to the invitation. You have to let the One who sent you the invitation know that you wish to come *and that you will be ready* when the day of the wedding arrives. Only then will a place be set for you at the table. If you do not respond to the invitation or you respond by actually declining the invitation, a place will not be set for you at the table of the wedding feast. The choice is left to each person to decide to follow Christ, or not.

Verse 10

> Then John falls at the feet of the angel to worship him, but the angel rebukes him and tells John not to do this as he (the angel) is a servant of God just like John and his brothers and sisters who testify about their faith in Jesus (i.e., all true believers). The angel tells John to worship only God, and that the essence of prophecy is to give a clear witness for Jesus.

John is then shown the vision of the long-awaited Second Coming of Christ, which we will now look at.

The Second Coming – God's prophesied Solution

Revelation 19:11-21: The Glorious Appearing of Christ, and the end of the Antichrist

Throughout this book, we have seen that the Antichrist leader (the beast) of a global alliance (the New World Order) has a sinister solution to solve the world's chaos. We have seen that this will become a reality, and he will succeed in his global domination. But the Lord has an ultimate solution concerning the Antichrist, which we will see in the following passage.

Below is the actual biblical text.

> "Then I saw heaven opened, and a white horse was standing there. Its rider was named Faithful and True, for he judges fairly and wages a righteous war. His eyes were like flames of fire, and on his head were many crowns. A name was written on him that no one understood except himself. He wore a robe dipped in blood, and his title was the Word of God. The armies of heaven, dressed in the

finest of pure white linen, followed him on white horses. From his mouth came a sharp sword to strike down the nations. He will rule them with an iron rod. He will release the fierce wrath of God, the Almighty, like juice flowing from a winepress. On his robe at his thigh was written this title: King of all kings and Lord of all lords.

Then I saw an angel standing in the sun, shouting to the vultures flying high in the sky: "Come! Gather together for the great banquet God has prepared. Come and eat the flesh of kings, generals, and strong warriors; of horses and their riders; and of all humanity, both free and slave, small and great.

Then I saw the beast and the kings of the world and their armies gathered together to fight against the one sitting on the horse and his army. And the beast was captured, and with him the false prophet who did mighty miracles on behalf of the beast—miracles that deceived all who had accepted the mark of the beast and who worshiped his statue. Both the beast and his false prophet were thrown alive into the fiery lake of burning sulfur. Their entire army was killed by the sharp sword that came from the mouth of the one riding the white horse. And the vultures all gorged themselves on the dead bodies." – Revelation 19:11–21 NLT

My comments: We know without a doubt that *this* rider on the white horse is Jesus, as He is Faithful and True, and He comes with the armies of heaven dressed in white robes who are also on white horses. Many people wonder who the 'armies of heaven' are. There are three views on their likely identity; the faithful believers taken by Jesus at the Rapture of the Church; the Tribulation saints, or the Old Testament saints. Whoever these armies of heaven consist of, Jesus will gather them from the four winds, from one end of the heavens to the other (see Matthew 24:31). He will give each of them a white horse to ride on and they will follow Him into the kingdom where they will rule and reign with Him for 1,000 years, judging the world (see 1 Corinthians 6:2).

For more information on this, go to https://studyingbibleprophecy. wordpress.com/2016/12/19/who-are-the-armies-that-will-follow-christ-on-white-horses/

This is the great battle of the global superpower alliance with its Antichrist leader (the beast), the false prophet (the Antichrist's assistant), and the kings and generals and strong warriors of the world against Jesus and the armies of heaven at the place called Armageddon (the Hebrew meaning is Mount Megiddo), previously referred to in Revelation 16.

In case anyone thinks that the battle of Armageddon is an event from a fictional horror story, in his book *The Last Hour – An Israeli Insider Looks at the End Times*, Amir Tsarfati shares something so incredible that it catapults this future prophesied event into reality;

'When I stand on the porch of my house, the Valley of Megiddo is spread out below me. The Bible calls it Armageddon – that infamous stretch of land where vast armies will assemble before marching to Jerusalem for the great final battle. It is hard to get the end times out of your mind when that valley is staring you in the face each day with your morning cup of coffee.' [1]

Despite this mass gathering of world leaders and their armies who are intent on destroying the Lord Jesus Christ, it will be a one-sided battle. God's *prophesied solution* is that the Antichrist and his false prophet will be thrown alive into the fiery lake of burning sulphur and their whole army will be killed by the sword that comes out of the mouth of the One riding on the white horse. We know from scripture that Jesus is the Word of God made flesh (see John 1:14), and also that the Sword of the Spirit is the Word of God (see Ephesians 6:17). Therefore, the sword that comes out of Jesus' mouth is the Word of God, and it is *this* Word that will destroy the beast's and the false prophet's entire army. However difficult this may be to comprehend and believe, it is the awesome truth of our almighty and supernatural God!

Revelation 20: The One Thousand Years, Satan's defeat, and the Final Judgement

Summary – Verses 1-3

With the Antichrist and the false prophet having been thrown into the lake of fire, and their entire army destroyed by the Word of God, an angel then binds Satan in chains for 1,000 years and throws him into the bottomless pit (Abyss), locking it so that he can no longer deceive the nations. This is for the duration of the 1,000 years reign of Christ and His followers on the earth.

My comments: We remember that it was Satan who gave his power to the beast (the Antichrist) and the false prophet to deceive the world. With both of them already in the lake of fire, it is now Satan's turn to head towards his ultimate end, firstly via the bottomless pit (the Abyss). However, after the 1,000 years are finished, Satan will be released for a short time, which we will see very shortly in the summary of verses 7-10.

Summary – Verses 4-6

John then sees people sitting on thrones who are given authority to judge. These are all the faithful ones who returned with Jesus on white horses. John sees the souls of all who have been beheaded for their faith, their testimony about Jesus, and proclaiming the Word of God. These are the ones who have not worshiped the beast or his statue and who have not accepted his mark on their right hand or their forehead. They are people who have come to faith in Christ *during* the Great Tribulation. All these souls (which had been beheaded for their faith in Jesus Christ) come back to life again and reign with Jesus for the 1,000 years. This is known as the first resurrection. Those who share in the first resurrection are blessed and holy because the second death holds no power over them. (The second death is the lake of fire, which we will see shortly in the summary of Revelation 20:11–15).

Then God's Word says that the rest of the dead will not come back to life until after Jesus' millennial reign is ended.

My comments: Many scholars believe 'the rest of the dead' refers to the wicked dead; those who refused to believe in Jesus Christ, and those who refused to repent of their sins. This would include people who professed faith in Christ but chose to continue in habitual sin, rejecting all godly teaching that one must repent of it. The wicked dead will be resurrected to face the final judgement, which will occur after Christ's millennial reign. Their souls will remain in the torment of Hades until they are resurrected to face the judgement seat of Christ. After the judgement, they will be cast into the lake of fire (see Revelation 20:15).

Summary – Verses 7-10

Initial comment: As we saw in Revelation 19:11–21, the beast (Antichrist) and his false prophet are thrown alive into the lake of fire, their entire army is destroyed by the Word of God from the mouth of Jesus. We saw above in Revelation 20:1-6 that Satan is at last bound in chains and thrown into the bottomless pit for 1,000 years whilst Christ is ruling and reigning the nations.

Verse 7

At the end of Christ's millennial reign, Satan is let out of the bottomless pit, but for one purpose only, which is to deceive all those from the nations called Gog and Magog. Satan will gather these people together from wherever they are around the world and surround the Lord's beloved city Jerusalem and His people.

My comments: Who are the people of Gog and Magog?

In Ezekiel 38:1-2, it says that Gog was a *person* of the land of Magog and was a prince who ruled over the nations of Meshech and Tubal. In Genesis 10:2 we find that Magog, Meshech, and Tubal were sons of Japheth (one of Noah's sons). As this is an End Times prophecy concerning Gog and Magog, these names could apply to people who are the *descendants* of Magog, Meshech, and Tubal. I would suggest reading Ezekiel chapters 38 and 39 in full to understand what God is going to do in this battle. For further information on who these nations might be, I would recommend reading Grant R. Jeffrey's book *Countdown to the Apocalypse,* which I have listed in the Recommended Reading at the end of this book.

But we need to remember that while this battle is waged against God's people and the city of Jerusalem, it is actually *Satan's* final attempt to destroy Jerusalem and those of the children of Israel who still remain on the earth. Satan knows that his own defeat is destined in this encounter, and that his ultimate end will be in the lake of fire, yet he still wants to deceive all who are left on the earth into thinking that he can succeed in his mission.

Summary – Verses 8-10

The size of Satan's army that will assemble for this final attempt will be as many as the grains of sand on the seashore. They will march across the earth and surround God's people and Jerusalem, but fire will come down from heaven and devour them. Satan will finally be thrown into the lake of fire, joining the Antichrist and his false prophet, where they will be tormented day and night forever and ever.

Summary – Verses 11–15: The Final Judgement

With the 1,000 years now passed and all the dead now raised (both the righteous and the unrighteous), John now sees a great white throne and the One who sits on it. All the dead, both great and small, are standing before God's throne, and books are opened, including the Book of Life.

"…And the dead were judged according to what they had done, as recorded in the books… All are judged according to their deeds." (Verses 12-13 NLT)

Death and the grave are thrown into the lake of fire. The lake of fire is the second death, and anyone whose name is not recorded in the Book of Life will be thrown into the lake of fire.

My comments: There will be no more death and so there will be no need for graves; hence, both death and the grave are also thrown into the lake of fire. There is no longer any need for either of them because the souls of all mankind will now live forever – either in the kingdom of heaven for true believers, *or* for eternity in the lake of fire for unbelievers and backslidden, unrepentant believers who refuse to forsake the sins they are allowing to remain in their lives.

Revelation 21: A New Heaven, a New Earth, and the New Jerusalem

Summary – Verses 1-27

Now that every form of evil has been thrown into the lake of fire, John is then shown the glory and beauty of the new heaven, the new earth and the New Jerusalem. It is full of the light of God and the Lamb. The gates are never shut, but nothing evil will be allowed to enter it. Only those whose names are written in the Lamb's Book of Life will be permitted entry. The New Jerusalem is colossal in its size. Its walls are two hundred and sixteen feet thick and the whole city is fourteen hundred miles in width, in length, and in height. That is a massive city! The walls are made of jasper and the city is pure gold, which is like glass in its appearance. The twelve foundation stones are laid with all sorts of precious stones, and the names of the twelve apostles are written on the foundation stones. The twelve gates are made from pearl and the street is made of pure gold that has the appearance of glass. Twelve angels guard the gates, and the names of the twelve tribes of Israel are written on the gates. This beautiful place is the inheritance of all true believers, where they will live for eternity. God will wipe away every tear from their eyes and there will be no more death or sorrow or crying or pain for all those who will live there; the ones whose names are written in the Lamb's Book of Life.

Revelation 22: The Conclusion of the Vision

Summary – Verses 1-6

John sees that the river of life flows from the throne of God and the Lamb down the centre of the main street. On each side of the river grows the tree of life, which bears a new crop of fruit each month. The leaves of these trees are used for healing the nations. The angel tells John that all the things he has seen are trustworthy and true. The angel concludes the vision by telling John that the Lord God, who inspires His prophets, *has sent His angel to tell His servants* (that is every Christian) *what will happen soon.*

My comments: So, this incredible End Times vision, recorded from the beginning of Revelation chapter 4 and culminating in the first part of Revelation chapter 22, is the angel of the Lord showing *us* through the Apostle John's faithful account, what will happen soon. The angel is saying that this prophetic vision of the End Times *is* trustworthy and true.

We need to believe it, every single bit of it, including what may happen to believers who have backslidden and turned away from obedience to the Lord and returned to their previous sinful lifestyles, and remain unrepentant. In some cases, what they turn back to can be even worse than what they did before (see 2 Peter 2:20). God's Word is the truth, the whole truth and nothing but the truth, so help us God.

Summary – Verses 7-10: Jesus is Coming Soon

Jesus speaks, saying,

> "Look, I am coming soon! Blessed are those who obey the words of prophecy written in this book." (verse 7 NLT)

> John again falls down at the feet of the angel to worship him, and again the angel rebukes him and tells him to worship only God. He is instructed to *'not seal up the prophetic words in this book, for the time* [of their fulfilment] *is near* (verse 10 AMP).

My comments: It would seem that the End Times prophecies given in the Old Testament to the prophet Daniel, which he was told to seal up for the time of the end (see Daniel 12:4), were again revealed to the Apostle John where the angel instructs John *not* to seal them up again. That would mean the End Times prophecies in the Book of Revelation are, at this moment in time, unsealed; they are open and ready to be fulfilled the moment God commands it.

Jesus speaks again, saying,

> "Look, I am coming soon, bringing my reward with me to repay all people according to their deeds. I am the Alpha and the Omega, the First and the Last, the Beginning and the End."

> Blessed are those who wash their robes. They will be permitted to enter through the gates of the city and eat the fruit from the tree of life. Outside the city are the dogs— the sorcerers, the sexually immoral, the murderers, the idol worshipers, and all who love to live a lie.

> **"I, Jesus, have sent my angel to give you this message for the churches.** I am both the source of David and the

heir to his throne. I am the bright morning star."

The Spirit and the bride say, "Come." Let anyone who hears this say, "Come." Let anyone who is thirsty come. Let anyone who desires drink freely from the water of life. And I solemnly declare to everyone who hears the words of prophecy written in this book: If anyone adds anything to what is written here, God will add to that person the plagues described in this book. And if anyone removes any of the words from this book of prophecy, God will remove that person's share in the tree of life and in the holy city that are described in this book.

He who is the faithful witness to all these things says, "Yes, I am coming soon!" Amen! Come, Lord Jesus!"
– Revelation 22:12–20 NLT (Author's emphasis)

My comments: I have emphasized some of Jesus' Words in the above passage because He says that He has sent His angel to give His message to the churches. That must therefore include the Church today. So why does the Church seem to be ignoring His message concerning the End Times and His warning of eternity in hell, in which many will find themselves?

It may be that many believers are too afraid to do any research about it in case they put themselves at risk of adding plagues to their life or having God remove their share in the tree of life and in the Holy City. Remaining in fear and ignorance is not what the Lord wants us to do. The Book of Revelation is God's Word. It is for us to read and study. Let us seek the Lord for wisdom and guidance regarding this vitally important subject, which is fast becoming a reality in our lifetime.

In His own words, Jesus says, *"I am coming soon!"* How soon? Only the Lord God knows. The angels don't know; not even Jesus knows (see Matthew 24:36). But nevertheless, Jesus is saying that He is coming soon. 'Soon' could be today, tomorrow, next week, next month, next year, or even many years ahead. No one knows;

only the Father...but we *must* be ready.

Conclusion: Let us honour our heavenly Father in reverential fear of His justice and His holiness, and worship Him by keeping watch for the return of our Bridegroom, His beloved Son, Jesus Christ, our Lord and Saviour so that we will be taken up with Him into heaven, escaping the wrath to come, and not find ourselves left behind on the earth to endure the Great Tribulation torment that will come upon the earth when the Antichrist arises.

EPILOGUE

The choice - Who will you follow?

"So fear the LORD and serve him wholeheartedly. Put away forever the idols your ancestors worshiped when they lived beyond the Euphrates River and in Egypt. Serve the LORD alone. But if you refuse to serve the LORD, then choose today whom you will serve. Would you prefer the gods your ancestors served beyond the Euphrates? Or will it be the gods of the Amorites in whose land you now live? But as for me and my family, we will serve the LORD." – Joshua 24:14-15 NLT

As we come towards the end of this book, I want to leave you with an urgent 'wake up' call. You have a choice to make which will have eternal consequences. The 'gods' of this world are all against Jesus Christ, and so, by this very fact, it means that they are all working for the kingdom of darkness whose leader is Satan, the Antichrist. If you reject Christ and choose to follow the things of this world, your choice means that you belong to the Antichrist, and unless you repent and give your life to Christ, it is clear from the Bible that everything I have written in this book - about the coming wrath of God upon all who are *not* followers of Christ - will befall you, and your eternal destiny will be in the lake of fire, along with Satan and all his demons (see Revelation 20:15).

But, like Joshua, in the passage above, if you will choose to serve the Lord wholeheartedly, putting your faith in Jesus Christ to save you, confessing and repenting of your sins and faithfully obeying the Word of God, you will receive eternal life in the kingdom of heaven, and will dwell in the House of the Lord forever.

God cannot make His message any clearer to you, and He used His servant Joshua to deliver it. Whilst this message was given to the Children of Israel, it also applies to the whole of the human race:

> "Now listen! Today I am giving you a choice between life and death, between prosperity and disaster. For I command you this day to love the LORD your God and to keep his commands, decrees, and regulations by walking in his ways. If you do this, you will live and multiply, and the LORD your God will bless you and the land you are about to enter and occupy.
>
> But if your heart turns away and you refuse to listen, and if you are drawn away to serve and worship other gods, then I warn you now that you will certainly be destroyed. You will not live a long, good life in the land you are crossing the Jordan to occupy.
>
> Today I have given you the choice between life and death, between blessings and curses. Now I call on heaven and earth to witness the choice you make. Oh, that you would choose life, so that you and your descendants might live! You can make this choice by loving the LORD your God, obeying him, and committing yourself firmly to him. This is the key to your life. And if you love and obey the LORD, you will live long in the land the LORD swore to give your ancestors Abraham, Isaac, and Jacob." – Deuteronomy 30:15-20 NLT

If you are not a follower of Christ, God has given you the free will to choose whom you will serve. I exhort you to choose Jesus Christ and be saved from the wrath to come and from the unfathomable torment that will last for eternity for all those who choose to follow the Antichrist and, at the last, find themselves cast into the lake of fire. Please read the **Addendum – A plea to unbelievers,** which follows this Epilogue.

If you are a follower of Christ, I urge you to not become complacent and comfortable about your life in Christ. It is so easy to drift along thinking that all is well with our soul, yet the way we live our life screams at us to the contrary. God used the prophet Joel to call His people, the Children of Israel, to repentance, and this most surely applies to us who are Gentile followers of Christ. What a powerful Word this is from the Lord, taken from the Amplified Bible translation:

"Even now," says the LORD,
"Turn and come to Me with all your heart [in genuine repentance],
With fasting and weeping and mourning [until every barrier is removed and the broken fellowship is restored];

Rip your heart to pieces [in sorrow and contrition] and not your garments."
Now return [in repentance] to the LORD your God,
For He is gracious and compassionate,
Slow to anger, abounding in lovingkindness [faithful to His covenant with His people];
And He relents [His sentence of] evil [when His people genuinely repent]." – Joel 2:12-13 AMP

As those who profess to be followers of Christ, let us humble ourselves and do what this passage of scripture exhorts us to do. No follower of Christ should be entertaining the idea of playing 'Russian Roulette' with their salvation; messing around in the fires of unrepentant sin, at risk of being left behind on the earth to endure the horrors of the Great Tribulation under the totalitarian control of the Antichrist. Jesus is coming back for His Bride; those who believe in Him and are faithfully and obediently living their lives in readiness for His appearing. They are alert and discerning of the signs of the times, and are watching, waiting, and listening out for the cry, *"...Behold, the bridegroom is coming...!"* (Matthew 25:6).

All of heaven is aware of the unfolding fulfilment of Bible prophecy as this world escalates towards the great Day of the Lord. But the generation to whom the End Time prophecies appear to relate, seems oblivious to it all. Instead of turning to Christ to save them from the distress of the worldwide chaos, they cling to the things of this fallen world in a desperate hope that the global nightmare they see on their television screens each day will vanish like the morning mist and their lives will return to normal as soon as possible.

In the same manner, the Bride of Christ (the Church) has never been so asleep. End Times events are materialising right in front of her eyes, but she appears to be in a coma. As believers, if we remain in this dangerous state, it is highly likely that our half-hearted and complacent attitude towards the return of the Bridegroom could result in the doors to the marriage of the Lamb and His Bride being shut in our faces. We may find ourselves calling to Jesus, saying, *"Lord! Lord! Open the door for us!"* (See Matthew 25:11), and He will reply to us with words that no Christian should ever want to hear, *"Believe me, I don't know you!"* (See Matthew 25:12).

As we approach the end of this book, J.C. Ryle gives us some profound words. Written over 100 years ago, may his powerful message, directed at both the Church and the world, penetrate deep into your soul and bring you to the realisation that no more time can be wasted being consumed by the things of this world. Only those who are ready will escape the terrifying rule of the Antichrist and the wrath of God which is coming. Only those who are ready for Jesus will go with Him into His kingdom. Time is running out, the Antichrist is arising, and Jesus could come for His Bride at any moment.

'Look at the rural parishes of such a land as ours, and think of them. See how the minds of the vast majority of their inhabitants are buried in farms and allotments, in cattle and corn, in rent and wages, in rates and tithes, in digging and sowing, in buying and selling, in planting and building. See how many there are who evidently care for nothing, and feel nothing, excepting the things of this world; who reckoned nothing whether their minister preaches law or gospel, Christ or antichrist, and would be utterly unconcerned if the Archbishop of Canterbury was turned out of Lambeth Palace, and the Pope of Rome put in his place. See how many there are of whom it can only be said that their bellies and their pockets are their gods. And then fancy the awful effect of a sudden call to meet the Lord Christ, a call to a day of reckoning, in which the price of wheat and the rate of wages shall be nothing, and the Bible shall be the only rule of trial! And yet remember, all this shall one day be.

Reader, picture these things to your mind's eye. Picture your own house, your own family, your own fireside. What will be found there? Picture above all your own feelings, your own state of mind. And then, remember, that this is the end towards which the world is hastening. There will be no long notice to quit. This is the way in which the world's affairs will be wound up. This is an event which may possibly happen in your own time.' [1]

Jesus exhorts us;

"Watch therefore, and pray always that you may be counted worthy to escape all these things that will come to pass, and to stand before the Son of Man." – Luke 21:36 NKJV

Solomon makes it absolutely clear what the whole human race should do and why;

"Now all has been heard;
here is the conclusion of the matter:
Fear God and keep his commandments,
for this is the duty of all mankind.
For God will bring every deed into judgment,
including every hidden thing,
whether it is good or evil." – Ecclesiastes 12:13-14 NIV

To all who have made it to the end of this book, I will leave you with this sobering thought…

We have been living in the last days since the time of Christ's ascension into heaven, but it now seems like we are living in the *last hours.*

With the sudden and unprecedented closure of churches worldwide due to Covid19, where many church leaders are afraid to open their doors again for fear of what may happen, and Christians being arrested, handcuffed and taken away by police officers for simply singing praises to God *outside* their church buildings, could it be that God is revealing to us that He is bringing the 'Church Age' - His 'Age of Grace' - to an end, in our lifetime? It is going to happen at some point, in fulfilment of Bible prophecy, and the End Times signs are all around us, blazing at us like emergency warning lights.

So, I ask you in all seriousness; are you ready for Christ's appearing? Are you ready for Him to come and rescue you out of this world and take you to be with Him in glory so that you will escape the reign of the Antichrist?

If not, I plead with you to do something about it *now.* The decision must be made *before* you die. None of us knows if God will grant us the gift of tomorrow…

ADDENDUM – A PLEA TO UNBELIEVERS

What must we do to be saved?

"Blow the trumpet in Zion [warning of impending judgment],
Sound an alarm on My holy mountain [Zion]!
Let all the inhabitants of the land tremble and shudder in fear,
For the [judgment] day of the LORD is coming;
It is close at hand…" – Joel 2:1 AMP

I have written this Addendum to show all unbelievers the inescapable reason why they need to turn to Jesus Christ to be saved; the critical point of this being to reveal the eternal destiny of those who reject God, but at the same time showing them the way of escape.

In the Beginning

As I showed you in Chapter 1, to know why salvation is essential to all of humanity, we need to understand and believe the eternal consequences of what happened to the first created humans, Adam and Eve. This account is written in Genesis chapters 1 to 4.

To summarize this again briefly, when God created Adam and Eve, they were created in His likeness, which would have been sinless perfection, knowing only how to do good and to please God. Everything that He created for them in the Garden of Eden was all for their use, but with one exception; God forbade them to eat the fruit of the tree of the knowledge of good and evil because He knew that if they ate of it, they would suddenly become aware of how to do things that are sinful and evil. But they were tempted by Satan to disobey God's command, and so they ate this forbidden fruit. At that moment their eyes were opened, and they realised what they had done. Because of their rebellion, God banished them from the Garden of Eden and posted cherubim at its gates to prevent them from ever entering it again.

Every person, since The Fall of Adam and Eve, has been born with the inherent disposition of that *original sin of rebellion against God's Word*. It is hardwired into our DNA. As a consequence of The Fall, the default position of every human being is that, after we die, we will spend eternity in hell because of our inherent sinful state. We all stand outside the 'Garden' (heaven) and something needs to happen to enable us to be made right with God so that we may enter in. We all need to be saved in order to receive eternal life in God's kingdom. Salvation has only been made available to us through Jesus Christ:

> "And there is salvation in no one else; for there is **no other name** under heaven that has been given among people **by which we must be saved [for God has provided the world no alternative for salvation].**" – Acts 4:12 AMP (Author's emphasis)

There is No Alternative

There is *no alternative* way to be saved, despite the multitude of bogus and deceptive claims of other spiritual organisations offering a spiritual path to salvation and eternal life by a means other than through faith in Jesus Christ. Such claims are an attempt to get into heaven through the wrong gate. The only gate to eternal life is through the narrow gate of faith in Jesus Christ and what He has accomplished on the cross for our salvation. Every other gate that is on offer by the world is a *counterfeit*, leading all who choose to go through those gates to end up in hell. Without faith in Jesus Christ *alone*, we will not be permitted entry into heaven. When we come to draw our last breath, if we have failed to believe and trust in Jesus for our eternal salvation, we will weep with much sorrow, regret and remorse.

Putting our trust in the false teachings of the alternative spiritual organisations of this world, which reject Jesus Christ's sacrifice on the cross, will not save us. Even if we are not following the teachings of other spiritual organisations but are simply living the best we can as 'good people', our good works on their own will not save us or allow us entry into heaven. Millions of people who do not have any kind of faith still think or hope that they will get into heaven or go to a 'better place' when they die, but the Word of God confirms that salvation is only through faith in Jesus Christ (see the scripture on the previous page and the one below).

> "For God so loved the world, that he gave his only Son, that whoever believes in him should not perish but have eternal life. For God did not send his Son into the world to condemn the world, but in order that the world might be saved through him. Whoever believes in him is not condemned, but whoever does not believe is condemned already, because he has not believed in the name of the only Son of God." – John 3:16-18 ESV

Fire! Fire!

If your house was on fire and someone showed you that there was *only one way* to escape and save your life, why would you refuse to follow that person to safety? Why would you choose to remain in the fire trying to find another way to save yourself, risking being burned alive in the flames? No one likes to think about hell, but it is a biblical reality. Jesus spoke about hell many times. The Apostle Peter told us what we need to do to be saved, and why (see Acts chapter 2). God's way of salvation through faith in Jesus Christ is the only way of escape from the raging fires of hell.

God doesn't want anyone to perish but *all* to come to repentance (see 2 Peter 3:9). When we come before the Lord in brokenness and godly sorrow over our sins, this leads us to repentance, and our repentance leads to our salvation (see 2 Corinthians 7:10).

May the message in this Addendum bring you to the place of confession, repentance and faith in Jesus Christ… as a matter of urgency.

Notes

Chapter 4

1. Ryle, J.C. *Are You Ready For The End Of Time? Understanding Future Events from Prophetic Passages of the Bible* Extracts from p.139. Christian Focus Publications Ltd, Geanies House, Fearn, Tain, Ross-shire IV20 1TW, Scotland, UK. Used by permission. www.christianfocus.com

2. ibid. p.29.

Chapter 5

1. Tsarfati, Amir, *The Last Hour – An Israeli Insider Looks at the End Times.* p.136. (Chosen Books, 11400 Hampshire Avenue South, Bloomington, Minnesota 55438). Used by permission. www.bakerpublishinggroup.com

2. ibid.

Chapter 6

1. Tsarfati, Amir, *The Last Hour – An Israeli Insider Looks at the End Times.* p.17. (Chosen Books, 11400 Hampshire Avenue South, Bloomington, Minnesota 55438). Used by permission. www.bakerpublishinggroup.com

Epilogue

1. Ryle, J.C. *Are You Ready For The End Of Time? Understanding Future Events from Prophetic Passages of the Bible* p.30. Christian Focus Publications Ltd, Geanies House, Fearn, Tain, Ross-shire IV20 1TW, Scotland, UK. Used by permission. www.christianfocus.com

Recommended Reading

1. Carter, J.W. *Trumpet Blast Warning*
    ISBN: 9780992795207

2. Ryle, J.C. *Are You Ready for the End of Time? Understanding Future Events from Prophetic Passages of the Bible*
    ISBN-13: 978-1857927474

3. Ryle, J.C. *Warnings to the Churches*
    ISBN: 9780851510439

4. Ryle, J.C. *Separation from the World*
    ISBN-13: 9781611045499

5. Ryle, J.C. *REPENTANCE*
    ISBN: 9781535339230

6. Ryle, J.C. *Heading for Heaven*
    ISBN-13: 9780852347102

7. Hill, Clifford, *The Reshaping of Britain – Church and State since the 1960s: A Personal Reflection*
    ISBN: 9780995683297

8. Tsarfati, Amir, *The Last Hour – An Israeli Insider Looks at the End Times*
    ISBN: 978-0-8007-9912-0

9. Jeffrey, Grant R. *The New Temple and the Second Coming*
    ISBN: 9781400071074

10. Jeffrey, Grant R. *Countdown to the Apocalypse*
    ISBN: 978-1-4000-744-19

11. Franks, Nicholas Paul, *BODY ZERO – Radical Preparation for the Return of Christ*
    ISBN: 978-1-78815-714-8

About the Author

After a powerful encounter with the Lord at a Good Friday church service in 1992, Michele's life was transformed from depression and suicidal thoughts to joy and thanksgiving that God had seen her, found her and given her the free gift of salvation and eternal life through faith in Jesus Christ. Within a month of this experience she was baptised by full immersion, filled with the Holy Spirit (as described in the Book of Acts chapter 2), and began witnessing to people on the streets. She has prayed for people and seen them miraculously healed, including personal healings for herself and her daughter.

Following a further encounter with the Lord in 2011, her life changed dramatically again, this time taking her into an area of ministry that she could never have imagined; that of writing books.

The burden she carries in her heart is to wake up followers of Christ from the dangerous slumber that has come upon the Church in the past 20 years. She urges believers to heed Jesus' teachings and warnings about unrepentant sin *within* the Church, and to be alert to the rise of false preachers who are teaching false gospels which are leading astray the flock throughout many denominations. Michele also exhorts believers to study what the Bible says about the End Times and to be watchful of the signs which will indicate the nearness of Christ's return.

When she is not writing, Michele enjoys immersing herself into her other God-given role as a full-time housewife. For rest and relaxation she enjoys photography, time out by the sea and visiting tea shops.

The Author's other books

Available on Amazon

Come on Church! Wake Up! – Sin Within the Church and What Jesus Has to Say About It

Paperback: ISBN: 978-1-62136-316-3

Kindle: ISBN: 978-1-62136-315-6

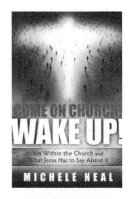

The End of The World and What Jesus Has to Say About It

Paperback: ISBN: 978-1-62136-742-0

Kindle: ISBN: 978-1-62136-743-7

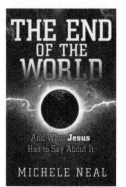

The Gospel of Deception – Counterfeit Christianity and the Fate of Its Followers

Paperback: ISBN: 978-1974387014

Kindle: ISBN: 1974387011

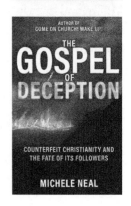

*When Healing Doesn't Happen –
A Life Lived for God through the
Journey of Suffering*

Paperback: ISBN: 978-1099706455

Kindle: ISBN: 1099706459

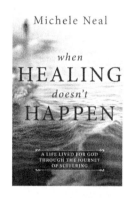

*Watchmen... or Wolves? – Demonic
Takeover in the House of God*

Paperback: ISBN: 9781671453661

Kindle: ISBN: B082SZTK89

Visit Michele's website www.michelenealuk.com

Follow Michele on Twitter @RaptureReadyUK

**If this book has impacted you, the author would be pleased if you
would consider writing a review for it on Amazon.**

Printed in Great Britain
by Amazon

41155465R00126